MARCONI: THE IRISH CONNECTION

BROADCASTING AND IRISH SOCIETY SERIES

Edited by Richard Pine

Marconi

The Irish connection

Michael Sexton

FOUR COURTS PRESS

Set in 10 on 13 point Janson Text by
Mark Heslington, Scarborough, North Yorkshire for
FOUR COURTS PRESS LTD
7 Malpas Street, Dublin 8, Ireland
e-mail: info@four-courts-press.ie
and in North America
FOUR COURTS PRESS
c/o ISBS, 920 N.E. 58th Avenue, Suite 300, Portland, OR 97213.

A catalogue record for this title
is available from the British Library.

ISBN 1-85182-840-0 hbk
ISBN 1-85182-841-9 pbk

Printed in Great Britain
by MPG Books, Bodmin, Cornwall.

Contents

Illustrations

Foreword

As the grandchild of someone who was employed at the headquarters of the Marconi Company at Chelmsford, England, before the first world war, and as a resident in Ireland where some of Marconi's most significant work was undertaken, I find a particular resonance in Michael Sexton's *Marconi: the Irish connection*. The fact that I never knew my grandfather (he died in 1917) has created an imaginative space in my awareness of the subject, not least because the penetrating gaze of his surviving photograph is so redolent of the many images of Marconi's own determined and self-confident posture. Living for much of the year in close proximity to Marconi's principal premises in Ireland – the transatlantic wireless transmitter at Derrygimla, near Clifden in Connemara – has increased both my imaginative and conceptual capacity for appreciating the significance of what Marconi did for Ireland and of what Ireland did for Marconi. Almost nothing remains of the Marconi station at Derrygimla, yet local folklore abounds in recollection of the station when operative, and of its dismantling and the plundering of its materials over many decades. Passing the site never fails to remind one that this empty space once accommodated the most advanced point-to-point wireless signalling station in the world, and that 'marconigrams' from Clifden once brought two sides of the world together in a previously unimaginable fashion, before the Irish civil war, and further technological advances, made its survival improbable.

The fact that Marconi was half Irish by virtue of his father's marriage to Annie Jameson, and the fact that he chose for his first wife Beatrice O'Brien, daughter of Lord Inchiquin of Dromoland Castle, is half the case for considering Marconi's Irish connection. The strategic geographical importance of Ireland at the start of the twentieth century, coupled with Marconi's extraordinary perception of the scientific possibilities of radio waves, is the other half. For a crucial few years, Marconi's insights as an electrical engineer became the fulcrum on which this Irish connection hinged and could be brought to fruition. At some of the most outlying parts of Ireland, from the northernmost part of the island – Malin Head and Rathlin – to its most eastern, western and southerly points (Dún Laoghaire, Clifden, Ballybunion and Crookhaven) Marconi's undertakings presented to the scientific community, and the economic and political worlds which it underpinned, advances in communications technology more complex and challenging than anything since the development of Reuter's telegraph system.

Michael Sexton combines the scientific knowledge of an expert in electrical engineering with a deep appreciation of what Marconi's technical experiments and achievements meant to Irish society. Marconi was more of a genius at spotting the potential that could be harnessed from the application of existing knowledge than he was an original inventor. Michael Sexton succeeds in placing Marconi's special skills of synthesis in the context of both Irish and international interest in, and contribution to, the developments of communications technology in a manner that elucidates clearly and uncompromisingly the reasons why we should, today, in a world which seems to have moved aeons away from these early developments, respect the long-standing significance and continuing relevance of Marconi's work. If nothing else, this book makes clear that, in addition to the ground-breaking work recognised in the award of the Nobel Prize to Professor Ernest Walton, there is at least one other scientist of Irish extraction on whom that same distinction has been conferred.

Richard Pine
Series Editor

For all my family

Acknowledgments

In a text, which has many different facets and ongoing developments, it is inevitable that an author has to draw on many sources. This is particularly the case in the present book since Marconi's many and varied activities in Ireland from 1898 to 1933 have, to the author's knowledge, never been assembled in a detailed and sequential manner between the covers of a single book or, at the very least, only the major operations were emphasised, e.g. the gigantic, transatlantic station at Clifden, Co. Galway.

Commencing with the Ballycastle-Rathlin Island link in 1898, A.D. (Barney) Patterson from Belfast and Martin Armour from Ballyclare, Co. Antrim were extremely helpful in acquainting me with the local scenes, whereas Ernest (Ernie) Shannon from Ballycastle itself at the Kenmara Hotel on the cliff top facing Rathlin was a mine of information and documentation since Marconi himself had carried out wireless transmissions from there. Professor Carson Stewart of Queen's University kept an interested eye on my search for relevant information. I must also acknowledge, with sincere gratitude the early encouragement of Professor Rosangela Barone, former director of the Italian Cultural Institute, Dublin.

Dr Sean Swords successfully searched the archives of Trinity College, Dublin for material on the academic successes of Edwin Glanville who was tragically and accidentally killed by falling from a cliff during the tests in 1898 on Rathlin soon after his arrival to take charge of the Marconi station on the East lighthouse. The author is deeply appreciative of the generosity of Jane Glanville and Patrick Glanville (a nephew of Edwin) in providing hitherto unknown letters from Edwin to his stepmother together with newspaper extracts relating to the tragedy on Rathlin. These letters cast significant new light on Edwin Glanville's important role with the Marconi Company both in England and Ireland. I also appreciate the introduction to the Glanville family by Sheila Stott, Schull, Co. Cork.

As regards the Crookhaven Station I would like to thank Suzanne Crosbie of the *Irish Examiner* for providing significant information concerning the telegraph service via ship from North America by Julius Reuter, which preceded

Marconi's wireless station by thirty-eight years. Clare Barrett of Marconi House, Crookhaven, where Marconi stayed during his visits, donated important documents, which had a significant bearing on the working of the station and its ultimate destruction. GEC Marconi Ltd, Chelmsford, forwarded a paper on the working of the Crookhaven Station in 1911: my thanks to Roy Rodwell for locating this in their archives.

The information provided by Mary Mackey, editor of the *Mizen Journal* and by Liam O'Regan, editor of the *Southern Star*, is also acknowledged.

Clifden station was, of course, the largest by far of Marconi's installations with an ancillary outlet at Ballybunion, Co. Kerry (a second ancillary was at Letterfrack but was not a success). Some years ago I visited both Clifden and Ballybunion – actually giving a lecture in Clifden – and had the pleasure of meeting Robert Jocelyn from Clifden and John O'Carroll in Ballybunion.

The co-operation of the Royal Irish Academy and the National Library of Ireland was also invaluable.

I have received a significant amount of original background information in Italy, notably at the University of Bologna (Professors Carlo Pancaldi and Anna Guagnini) and at the Fondazione Guglielmo Marconi (Dr Barbara Valotti). Furthermore, a display of actual-size working models of Marconi's original circuits of incredible accuracy was demonstrated to me by Maurizio Bigazzi – a real bonus. Professor Carlo Someda of the University of Padova has kindly read the script, suggesting various alterations to give overall improvement. Princess Elettra Marconi, Marconi's youngest daughter, has also shown a lively interest in the book.

The author is also grateful to Professor Gerard Wrixon, President of the National University of Ireland, Cork, for providing the facilities to carry out the work and to Professor Patrick Murphy also of NUI, Cork for reading the manuscript with the appropriate positive comments. The interest and encouragement of Peter Feeney, Head of Public Affairs Policy, RTÉ and of the series editor Richard Pine is very much appreciated. The patience and understanding of the staff of Four Courts Press, especially Martin Fanning, and the secretarial assistance of Adrienne Bray are gratefully acknowledged.

I am also indebted to the following organisations for permission to reproduce diagrams, photographs, etc. which appear in the text: Editore Giorgio Mondadori, Milan; European Broadcasting Union, Geneva; Institution of Electrical Engineers, London; Kangaroo Press, Kenthurst, New South Wales; Northern Ireland Tourist Board; Oxford University Press; Samton Ltd, Maynooth; Wolfhound Press, Dublin.

Finally, the painstaking proof-reading and general comments on the whole book by my wife, Leonore, are to be especially noted in sincere appreciation.

CHAPTER 1

Introduction

With the current massive worldwide expansion in communications (digital radio and television, satellites, information technology, telephony etc.) we may be inclined to overlook Ireland's rôle in some of the very earliest mass communications experiments carried out in this country just over a century ago.

Ballycastle, Rathlin, Kingstown (Dún Laoghaire), Crookhaven, Malin Head, Rosslare, Clifden, Letterfrack and Ballybunion became household names within the rapidly expanding wireless telegraph industry which was beginning to make serious inroads into the established wire telegraph networks which, dating from the 1840s with the onset of the railways, had been pioneered by such distinguished electrical scientists (or electricians as they were called at the time) as Samuel Morse, Charles Wheatstone and Isambard Brunel. In fact, the nineteenth century witnessed the emergence of the three great methods of transmitting information over realistic distances: wire telegraphy (Ronald, London, 1816), telephony (Bell, New Jersey 1876) and wireless (Marconi, Bologna 1895). All in all, there was, as a contemporary financial source remarked in London in the early 1900s 'a massive flutter in the dovecots of telegraphy'.

Irish links with the birth of wireless communications may, perhaps, be fading into obscurity at this stage but the name and fame of the Irish-Italian pioneer, Guglielmo Marconi, is permanently enshrined in the history of wireless as he was the prime mover in establishing and operating wireless facilities at all of these locations in Ireland, starting from 1898. He is still recalled by the descendants of people who were either employed in, or lived around, his stations during his many sojourns in Ireland.

Marconi is credited with having had the first paid job in radio when he made the first wireless link for shipping under contract from Lloyds of London between Ballycastle and Rathlin Island, Co. Antrim in 1898. Also in 1898, Marconi made the first ever journalistic use of wireless when he transmitted over the high seas more than 700 messages on the progress of the Kingstown Regatta to a waiting crowd of 20,000 in Dublin. One can imagine the chagrin, delight and general chaos in the heady atmosphere of the bookmakers' offices as the regatta results were being posted up on the newspaper office windows.

In the summer of 1901, using the newly commissioned shipping commercial station at Crookhaven, Co. Cork, Marconi received strong and clear signals from his station at Poldhu, Cornwall – a distance of 225 miles – which confirmed that the radio waves followed the curvature of the earth. This was a crucial test for his great gamble of successfully bridging the Atlantic in December 1901 between Cornwall and Newfoundland, leading directly to the massive transatlantic station at Clifden, Co. Galway, in 1907.

Clifden was the world's first fixed point-to-point morse telegraphy station, sending 'marconigrams' to the new world. With reduced charges and higher transmission rates, this really 'rattled' the telegraph companies and the pigeons began to abandon the dovecots. A further claim to fame was that Clifden's ancillary station at Ballybunion, Co. Kerry was the location for the first east-to-west transatlantic speech and music transmission in 1919, this advancement being made possible by the introduction of thermionic valves to the circuits. By this time Marconi was universally accepted as the 'Father of Wireless Telegraphy', whereas the Canadian physicist R.H. Fessenden, who had been working on voice transmission as early as 1903, was recognised as the 'Father of Wireless Telephony'. Incredibly, Fessenden had transmitted gramophone records to ships 80km from the coast in 1906, arguably the first wireless broadcast. Marconi, of course, with his usual sharp eye to business, followed up the Ballybunion test with a full-blown radio broadcast in 1920 from a studio/transmitter in Chelmsford, UK, of the famous operatic soprano, Dame Nellie Melba. By 1922 he had secured contracts for the newly emerging BBC and, as we shall see, installed the first transmitters for Radio Éireann in 1926 and 1933.

Marconi's marriage to Beatrice O'Brien was a tempestuous affair but it did survive until a mutually agreed and amicable divorce in the north-eastern Italian city of Fiume in 1924. There were two daughters and one son from this marriage, with the eldest daughter Degna publishing a very readable and detailed biography of her father in Italian and English in which his activities in Ireland (which she visited with him occasionally) are given significant prominence. In 1927, Marconi married Maria Cristina Bezzi-Scali, descended from an ancient aristocratic family originating from the Ravenna–Bologna area. Her father was a papal count with considerable influence in the inner circles of the Vatican, and it was no surprise that Marconi was subsequently awarded the contract for a VHF radio link between Vatican City and the papal summer residence at Castelgandolfo in 1932 – yet another 'first' for Marconi internationally.

It is still occasionally remarked that Marconi himself did not invent anything worthwhile but that he had simply 'picked other people's brains'. A glance at the Chronology (p. 19) clearly shows the considerable advances in the understanding of electricity and magnetism in the late eighteenth and throughout the nineteenth century. Marconi, who had attended the Istituto Nazionale at

Livorno, also had private tuition in physics from Professor Vincenzo Rosa, who was attached to a 'liceo' at Livorno and, in addition, was taught by a neighbour of the family at the Villa Griffone – Professor Augusto Righi, Bologna University – where he was given the freedom of the library and laboratories. In particular, during 1894–5, Marconi read an account of a lecture in London given by Oliver Lodge commemorating the untimely death of Heinrich Hertz. Lodge successfully demonstrated wireless transmission over approximately twenty-five metres between lecture theatres. Marconi, then only twenty years of age, could scarcely believe that the enormous potential of telegraphy without wires had not been grasped, especially as most, if not all, of the constituent components were already available. Lodge himself subsequently admitted that he was too busy with university teaching and administration at Liverpool to give the matter much thought, even though he had just developed the syntonic, tuned circuit (see below). Marconi immediately commenced experiments on his father's estate, Villa Griffone, fifteen kilometres from Bologna and, within six months, succeeded in transmitting over several kilometres.

He had an uncanny ability to adapt the original research of other scientists to his own requirements. For example, Eduard Branly of the Institute Catholique, Paris had been the first to develop the coherer detector of electromagnetic waves in the 1880s and Marconi subsequently improved its performance out of all recognition, also developing the magnetic detector (affectionately known as the 'Maggie') from the research of Rutherford himself. The late Professor Ernest Walton of Trinity College, Dublin, and joint Nobel Prize winner with Sir John Cockcroft for the atom-splitting experiment of 1932, told this author that Marconi had visited him in Cambridge to view his high voltage power supply for possible improvements to his own transmitter circuits.

Marconi also employed high-level consultants to perfect his systems. Foremost amongst these was Professor Ambrose Fleming of London, the inventor of the thermionic diode in 1904, which, ultimately, became an integral component of transmitters as a power rectifier and of receivers as a sensitive detector. He also assisted in the designs of the various antenna systems, especially the directional type which was vital for the Clifden transatlantic link. Thomas Round, developer of the Round-Travis Frequency Modulated (FM) detector was also employed by Marconi during his later worldwide shortwave transmissions.

Perhaps the most controversial consultant was none other than Oliver Lodge who, as part of an extremely hard bargain made with Marconi regarding the sale of his tuned circuit patent for the huge sum then valued at £10,000 stg [today, €530k] also forced Marconi to hire him as a consultant for several years The technical situation was acute since the ever increasing proliferation of spark transmitters made receiver sensitivity an absolute requirement, especially relating to safety at sea (lighthouses, ship-to-ship and ship-to-shore communications).

Figure 1.1 Marconi's interests in Ireland

Obviously Lodge had learned his lesson about being too busy with teaching. This was one of the few lapses made by Marconi but it caused considerable financial problems for some time and indeed but for the coming into operation of the Clifden transatlantic station in 1907, and the fact that Marconi a wireless on board the ill-fated *Titanic* prevented an almost total disaster in 1912, the

Marconi Wireless Telegraph Co. would in all probability have gone into bankruptcy.

It will be clear that Marconi was what we would now describe as a superb 'systems' engineer. This, coupled with a sharp business acumen, boundless energy and, most importantly, his ability to 'get on' with both scientific and financial colleagues ensured that almost every development that he pioneered was ultimately successful.

The text of this book is structured to facilitate the general non-scientific reader with an interest in the spectacular achievements of Marconi in the field of wireless telegraphy over 100 years ago.

The newspaper article in Appendix 1 by Professor George Fitzgerald explains in a masterly fashion the 'Meaning and Possibilities of Wireless Telegraphy' for an Irish readership which, in common with other nationalities, had little knowledge of the topic in 1898. The other four appendices are also reproduced from original sources: Callan (1836), Preece (1897) and Marconi himself (1905) together with his Nobel lecture (1909). Although technical in nature, these papers are also directed towards a scientific community still largely unacquainted with the new developments in electromagnetism.

Chronology of the evolution of wireless telegraphy in the eighteenth and nineteenth centuries

	SCIENTIST	CONTRIBUTION
1770	Cavendish (Cambridge), Coulomb (Paris)	Static Electric Charges
1790	Galvani (Bologna), Volta (Pavia)	Electric Currents
1820	Oersted (Copenhagen), Ampère (Paris)	Electric Currents, Magnetic Fields
1831	Faraday (London)	Electromagnetic Induction
1836	*Callan (Maynooth)	Induction Coil (Transformer)
1842	Henry (Princeton)	Induction Experiments
1964	Maxwell (Edinburgh)	Electromagnetic Theory
1866	Loomis (Virginia)	Wireless Demonstration
1879	Hughes (London)	'Wireless' Demonstration
1882	*Fitzgerald (Dublin)	Proposal to check Maxwell's Theory
1888	Hertz (Karlsruhe)	Experimental Verification of Maxwell's Theory
1890	Righi (Bologna)	Spherical Oscillators (Transmitters)
1890	Branly (Paris)	Receiver Coherer
1893	Tesla (Prague)	Wireless Patent / HF Alternators
1894	Lodge (Liverpool)	Syntonic (Tuned) Circuits
1895	Marconi (Bologna)	EM Wave Transmission and Reception
1895	Popov (St Petersburg)	EM Wave Reception
1898	Marconi (in Ireland)	Commercial Radio Link

* The contributions of the Revd Nicholas Callan from St Patrick's College, Maynooth, who developed the Induction Coil and of George F. Fitzgerald from Trinity College, Dublin, for his foresight in clearly seeing the potential applications of Maxwell's theory are to be noted. In fact, it is recorded that Fitzgerald was present at Marconi's wireless test at Kingstown in 1898 (see text) and that an induction coil fabricated by Callan was used in those tests.

The reader will have noticed the origins of the various units of electromagnetism from some of these names. For example, those in everyday usage are:

Volta	Electrical voltage, V (volt)	Faraday	Electrical capacitance, Farad, C
Ampère	Electrical current, I or A (amp)	Henry	Electrical inductance, Henry, H
Hertz	Electrical frequency, Hz		

1865

AMERICA.
(REUTER'S TELEGRAMS.)

GREAT   BATTLES.

RICHMOND TAKEN

OCCUPATION BY GRANT.

GREAT CAPTURE OF PRISONERS

ARRIVAL OF THE AUSTRALASIAN.
(*Via* CROOKHAVEN.)

The following are the heads of the news brought by the Australasian :—

NEW YORK, APRIL 5 (NOON).

After three days' bloody battle Grant occupied Richmond and Petersburg on Monday morning. Lee retreated north of the Appomattox in the direction of Lynchburg, closely pursued by Grant, who was capturing numbers of prisoners along the route.

Correspondents estimate Lee's loss at 15,000 killed and wounded, 25,000 prisoners, and from 100 to 200 guns.

Grant's losses are 7,000 men.

Gold, 148¾.

NEW YORK, APRIL 5 (NOON).

Official reports from General Grant to President Lincoln received on Sunday announced that severe and bloody fighting had been progressing around Richmond during Friday, Saturday, and Sunday. At noon on Monday it was officially announced that Petersburg had been evacuated, and that General W...

April 14th.

Historic cablegram relating to the final days of the American Civil War, processed at Crookhaven

CHAPTER 2

The Marconi ancestry

Guglielmo Marconi: how a genius was born – rural origins and the ascent of the family
The Marconi name is thought to have originated in the fifteenth or sixteenth century in the town of Granaglione, approximately thirty kilometres south west of Bologna, the principal city of the province of Reggio Emilia in Central Italy. This rather sketchy information was first referred to in a population census of 1700.[1] The actual name signifies the 'descendants of Marco' (*i discendenti di Marco*) to distinguish it from others of the same name in accordance with the tradition of rural society of the time to call individuals after paternal or maternal names or, indeed, some original distinguishing family feature such as the original location.

From Granaglione the Marconi families gradually spread throughout the region as evidenced by the censuses taken during the nineteenth century. In particular, it was recorded in the census of 1848 in the small village of Capugnano, high in the Appenines, that the Marconi families now numbered six, amounting to twenty-three individuals involved in farming, bricklaying and general labour. In addition, although not officially registered at Capugnano, Domenico and Giuseppe Marconi, grandfather and father respectively of Guglielmo, were born there.

Towards the middle of the nineteenth century, two distinct Marconi family branches were emerging: the Capugnano branch (near Poretta) and the other at Varano (near Granaglione), presided over by Dionigi Marconi, to whom Guglielmo would almost certainly have been a distant cousin; Dionigi's brother was, in fact, a working-class joiner, highlighting that this branch of the family had begun its ascent into society.

Let us pause for a moment to illustrate the type of life led by the Marconi clan at Capugnano a century and a half ago. The winters were harsh in these high mountains which was reflected in an austere and hardy people who worked the land raising oats and maize in small and stubborn fields using wood fuel of birch

---

1 A. Giacomelli, G. Bertocchi, *Guglielmo Marconi, Come Nasce un Genio: Le Origini Montane e l'Ascesa della Famiglia* (Bologna: Nuèter – Ricerche, 1994), p. 161ff.

and fir cut from the rocky slopes. By a judicious series of land acquisitions (assisted without doubt by their legal cousin Dionigi) the Marconis had effectively become 'landed gentry' in this remote and almost inaccessible region, living frugally in the thin yet luminous air on their holdings which, at this stage, extended from Capugnano to the larger town of Poretta. In Poretta itself the Marconi name is still visible, etched on the back of one of the chestnut pews in the old church.[2]

Although not rich by urban standards the Marconis possessed the arrogant self-reliance endemic in such a largely illiterate countryside and the habit of command was in their blood together with a somewhat obstinate, prickly, yet sensitive nature coupled with not inconsiderable courage. These particular characteristics surfaced subsequently in a most remarkable fashion in the most illustrious member of the clan – Guglielmo.

Giuseppe was educated by priests as there was some hope that he would enter the Church but it soon became obvious that he had no vocation. However, his younger and far more God-fearing brother Arcangelo – later randomly murdered by a thief – did take holy orders whereas Giuseppe concentrated on the management of his father's properties.

Giuseppe's general outlook was far more worldly than the priesthood and, inevitably, Capugnano and Poretta became too restricted for his ambition and he became the first member of this Marconi family to leave the hills. At the age of twenty-five in 1852 he moved to Bologna, still near enough to enable him to see the mountainous country he had abandoned on the horizon beyond the plain of Emilia.

The social advance of the Marconi families from primitive and remote peasantry which arose from successive land acquisitions, education, direct connection with the Church through the unfortunate Arcangelo, and with the law through cousin Dionigi bears a remarkable resemblance to the situation pertaining to rural Ireland until recently. Accordingly, by the time Giuseppe arrived in Bologna, he was able to expand his activities both socially and economically. This enabled him to be accepted in Bologna as a member of the lower middle class (*la piccola Borghesia*) with its usual and inevitable related prejudices.

In the course of his social activities in Bologna Giuseppe met and ultimately married Giulia de Renoli in 1855. Her parents were bankers. However, tragedy struck within a year when Giulia died in childbirth having borne Giuseppe a son. Giuseppe of course, was devastated and sent for his aged and lonely father Domenico Marconi, who sold his properties at Poretta and came to Bologna. However, the city proved too much for the old mountaineer who soon bought

---

2 Degna Marconi, *My Father Marconi* (London: Frederick Muller, 1962), Part I; also published in Italian: *Marconi, mio Padre* (Milan: Frasinelli, 1993).

Figure 2.1 16th-century house of Marconi at Granaglione near Bologna

an estate at Pontecchio, 15 km from Bologna. This was the now-famous Villa Griffone surrounded by rolling fields and vineyards. Here old Domenico enjoyed his last few years tending his property and, when he died, Giuseppe inherited the estate and spent most of his time there, a widower very much alone except for the young son Luigi.

Annie Jameson and Giuseppe Marconi
In the words of Degna Marconi, Guglielmo's eldest daughter writing in 1962, 'Annie Jameson was a pretty girl from Ireland with a glorious singing voice and a will of her own'.[3] It was her voice that brought her to Italy to study '*bel canto*', the trip offered as consolation by her family because they had forbidden her to accept an engagement to sing at Covent Garden Opera House.

Annie was from the Jameson clan of Scottish Presbyterian stock who had come to Ireland in the late eighteenth century and established distilleries in Dublin and Enniscorthy. Andrew Jameson, while in Enniscorthy, had four daughters and the family lived in an old manor, Daphne Castle. Bearing in mind the Scottish background, a career in opera for their youngest daughter was quite unthinkable, especially in the 1800s.

When Annie arrived in Bologna to study at the Accademia Musicale or

3 Ibid.

Figure 2.2 Annie Marconi with Guglielmo (l) and Alfonso (r)

Conservatorio, she stayed with business colleagues of her family who turned out
to be none other than the de Renolis, the same bankers whose daughter Giulia
had died in childbirth after a one-year marriage to Giuseppe Marconi, their son-
in-law. Apparently it was love at first sight between Annie and Giuseppe and
Annie, abandoning the '*bel canto*' without hesitation, went back home to ask her
parents' permission to marry her Italian.

   Annie must have been a super-optimist because in the view of her parents, just
about everything was unsuitable about Giuseppe; he was a widower with one
child, there was an age difference of seventeen years and there were religious
differences, but worst of all he was a foreigner. This was far too much for the

conservative semi-Victorian Scottish-Irish Jamesons who were quite literally outraged, convinced that Annie could not have made a more disastrous choice. Permission was refused and Annie bowed so gracefully to her parents' objections that they thought that this was the end of the affair.

What they did not realise was that Giuseppe in his Italian villa and Annie in her Irish castle were smuggling letters to each other and waiting until she came of age. At that stage Annie went down through England and across the English Channel by ship, while Giuseppe traveled up by coach, meeting each other in Boulogne-sur-mer. They were married there on 16 April 1864, then travelled straight to Bologna across the Alps. This was indeed a romantic affair, certainly more exciting than Victorian fiction.

Annie immediately took Bologna to her heart, recognising the fundamental elegant beauty of this Renaissance city and was even more impressed when Giuseppe told her that he had taken a town house for the winter in the city itself.

One year after the romantic elopement, about which no sharp objection appeared to have come from Annie's parents who, after all, would have been pragmatic business people, Annie and Giuseppe's first child was born in the Villa Griffone; the boy was named Alfonso. Nine years elapsed before Annie had another child.

This occasion initially seemed to be almost a repeat of the tragedy of Giuseppe's first wife, since Annie had an extremely life-threatening delivery – indeed at one stage matters looked very serious indeed for her – but on the morning of 25 April 1874 a second son was safely born and christened Guglielmo. Within twenty-five years the era of wireless telegraphy would be securely established as a result of this birth.

Guglielmo's parents being utterly different in virtually every sense of the word, it is worthwhile to see which characteristics he had inherited from them. We have already noted the dour, independent aloofness of mountain people coupled with strong fortitude, all of which Guglielmo subsequently showed. Another major feature was an ability to make do with what is available, this being a crucial feature of Marconi's wireless experimentation since he literally improvised most of his own equipment as he progressed in the initial stages. From his mother he inherited a will as stubborn as his father's but this was tempered with music, poetry and grace. He became a serious patron of the arts both in England and Italy and was responsible for sponsoring the famous Irish operatic soprano Margaret Burke Sheridan for tuition in Rome (see Chapter 10). He also inherited his mother's blue eyes and fair hair (some would say that this was from her Q-Celtic background) and these characteristics were passed on to his own youngest daughter Elettra.

CHAPTER 3

Marconi – the early years
in Italy and England

Early education in Italy

> In sketching the history of my association with Radiotelegraphy I might
> mention that I never studied Physics or Electro technics in the regular
> manner, although as a boy I was deeply interested in those subjects. I did,
> however, one course of lectures on Physics under the late Professor Rosa at
> Livorno, and I was, I think I might say, fairly well acquainted with the publi-
> cations of that time dealing with scientific subjects including the works of
> Hertz, Branly and Righi.[1]

These are Marconi's own words, delivered in his Nobel Lecture before the Royal
Academy of Science in Stockholm in December 1909, when he accepted the
Nobel Prize in Physics which he shared with the German physicist Dr Ferdinand
Braun. The prize-sharing with Braun occasioned surprise, if not some resentment,
on the part of Marconi which was not totally unjustified since his spectacular
achievements in Radio Science far outweighed the work of Braun. The international academic politics of Nobel prize awards was, and still is, legendary.[2]

   Almost from the time he was born, Marconi's strong-willed mother Annie was
determined to instil her own Scots-Irish background into the growing boy, to
balance the Catholic and Italian ancestry of his father Giuseppe. She actually
brought him to England when he was just five years old and he stayed there for
several years, immersed in the English-speaking world. On his return to Italy the
young Marconi spoke indifferent Italian with an English-Irish accent and was
ridiculed at school not only by his fellow pupils but also by some of his teachers;
'Guglielmo, your Italian is dreadful!' This upset Guglielmo considerably and he
tended to withdraw into himself. It was compounded later by the somewhat
hostile attitude of his father towards his initial wireless experiments at the Villa
Griffone, leading him to depend even more on his mother.

---

1 G. Marconi, *Nobel Lecture*, Royal Academy of Science, Stockholm, 11 December 1909. **2** P. Rowland,
'The Nobel Prize: some cautionary tales', *History of Physics Newsletter*, No. 15 (Institute of Physics, London
2002), p. 67.

Giuseppe intended to hand over management of the family estate to his sons Alfonso and Guglielmo. The role of Luigi, his son by his first marriage, appears to be somewhat unclear in this allocation. However, Giuseppe, who was probably influenced by Annie, was not inflexible about this and had no major objection to his sons undertaking studies to prepare themselves for a professional career. The two young brothers did not, in fact, have a regular scholastic education and, up to 1885, had private lessons usually augmented by Annie herself. One of the major obstacles to a traditional course of study was their frequent excursions with Annie. The Villa Griffone at Pontecchio was only 15 km from Bologna and Annie was in the habit of spending long winter periods elsewhere, especially at Livorno and Florence. One of the major attractions of these two cities, apart from the better climate which was beneficial for Annie's health, was that both Livorno and Florence had a significant number of English expatriates at that time. In particular, Livorno was also an important international maritime centre and a staging base for commercial and military traffic between Britain and its colonies (this was before the Boer War when the British Empire under Queen Victoria was at its peak). Furthermore Annie's sister, who was married to an English general in the Indian Army, actually lived in Livorno.

When, towards his twelfth year, Guglielmo began to follow with regularity a study course to obtain the *licenza elementare*, a private school in Florence was chosen for him. In the following year; however, he transferred to Livorno where he registered in the Istituto Nazionale. It was during the study period in this latter school between 1891 and 1892 that he became increasingly interested in experimental science. His enthusiasm was such that he persuaded his parents to enhance the programme offered by the Istituto with private lessons, and this was entrusted to Vincenzo Rosa, professor of physics in a *liceo* in Livorno. Rosa, a graduate in physical science and mathematics from Turin University, was famous not only for excellent teaching but also for skilful experimentation.

Marconi afterwards observed that it was the remarkable interest of Rosa in electricity which had guided him towards that particular field of study. On the other hand it is easy to understand the reason why Marconi chose electrical phenomena as his field of interest since by that time, towards the end of the nineteenth century, it was beginning to become clear that electricity had enormous potential for further applications in addition to those already achieved. The extraordinary successes with the telegraph in the mid-ninetenth century by, among others, Wheatstone and Morse, had not ceased to astonish the general public as electrical illumination was introduced, followed by the construction of large electrical power stations. In the view of contemporaries, electricity became synonymous with progress and seemed a Pandora's Box, able to produce virtually an infinite number of scientific and practical solutions to various problems.

Applications in metallurgy, industrial chemistry, transport and medicine come to mind and giants such as Hughes (electric printing press), Edison (electric lighting) and Tesla (alternators) are examples of specific inventions with universal applications.

After Michael Faraday and Jean-Marie Ampère had impressed their contemporaries in the years between 1820 and 1840, by establishing the connection between electricity and magnetism, James Clerk Maxwell, working between 1865 and 1879, established a set of equations which ultimately led to the proposal of electromagnetic waves propagating at the speed of light which itself was electromagnetic, differing from conventional radio only in frequency or wavelength. The famous experiment of Heinrich Hertz in 1888 verified Maxwell's proposals in a convincing manner. Other experimentalists soon followed, namely Eduard Branly (coherer detector), Oliver Lodge (tuning/syntony) and Augusto Righi (spark transmitter). All these physicists explored the characteristics and properties of the phenomena that Maxwell had described in his equations. It will also be noted that Hertz, Branly and Righi are also mentioned in the opening paragraphs of Marconi's Nobel Lecture at the beginning of this chapter. Marconi did not seem to value Lodge's contributions very highly although he had, in fact, developed and patented the first resonant circuit in 1893 and subsequently delivered the famous lecture commemorating Hertz in 1894 which excited great interest from Marconi.

Augusto Righi, appointed Professor of Physics at Bologna University in 1889, was considered to be one of the best experimentalists in Italy. He was a neighbour of Annie Jameson who introduced Guglielmo to him as soon as she could since Righi had a keen interest in electromagnetism. Guglielmo discussed his ideas frequently with Righi who initially thought that he was operating above his status as a mere dilettante who was not even eligible on educational grounds to register as a student at Bologna and, moreover, had failed an entrance test for the Italian Navy. However, the young Marconi convinced Righi of his natural intelligence so that Righi allowed him to work in his laboratory and also made the University Library available to him. It is likely also that Marconi assisted Righi with his experiments which included optimisation of the spark transmitter which was an essential element in Marconi's first experiments.

Some very interesting information has recently come to light concerning Marconi's activities *before* he began his wireless tests in 1895. In 1892 he erected apparatus on the roof of the house in Livorno to make a survey of atmospheric electricity (naturally occurring sparks or lightning). He also experimented with various types of electrical batteries. Although little evidence remains of these experiments, some hitherto unknown and unedited notebooks by Marconi have recently been discovered in the archives of the Accademia del Lincei in Rome, describing in his own handwriting some of his 'dilettante experimentation' during 1891 and 1892.[3]

From these exercise books it appears that Marconi not only spent much time at these researches but also appears to have had more than enough funds at his disposal, presumably provided by his mother. The notes are quite detailed and Marconi used existing scientific measuring instruments as a guide for his own designs: perhaps Marconi's efforts are best summarised by a letter sent to his brother Alfonso in 1892 referring to the construction of a thermoelectric battery:

> My electrical studies are proceeding very well with very satisfactory results both from theoretical and industrial aspects and I am certain that the final device that I have fabricated will merit an industrial monopoly.[4]

Note the confidence of this extract. Presumably the word 'monopoly' implies a patent. In reality the results were not quite as positive and the young inventor eventually abandoned the project. Nevertheless, it was a clear indication that, several years before he commenced his wireless experiments, Marconi was fully aware of the importance of obtaining legal recognition for the priority of his inventions and all this at the age of eighteen years.

Marconi's wireless propagation experiments at the Villa Griffone, 1895
In 1894 Oliver Lodge had given a memorial lecture in commemoration of Heinrich Hertz who had died prematurely at the age of thirty-six in the same year. Entitled *The Work of Hertz and Some of his Successors* at the Royal Institution, London, it was widely reported and finally appeared as part of a book that went into several editions.[5]

The lecture included demonstrations of 'telegraphy without wires' during which electromagnetic transmissions were successfully accomplished between adjoining rooms – a distance of tens of metres. Marconi happened to read an account of this lecture, possibly in Professor Righi's library, and it made an instant and everlasting impression on him.

Marconi himself had a feeling of near disbelief that no one had grasped the commercial possibilities of Hertzian waves. 'When I started my first experiments with Hertzian waves', he is quoted as saying, 'I could scarcely believe it possible that their application to useful purposes could have escaped the notice of eminent scientists'.[6]

It is very instructive at this stage to describe the sensational experiment of

3 A. Guagnini, I.G. Pancaldi: *Cento Anni di Radio: Le Radici dell'invenzione* (Turin, SEAT, 1995).   **4** Ibid.
5 O.J. Lodge, *Signalling through Space without Wires: The Work of Hertz and His Successors* (London: Electrician Printing and Publishing Co., 1894).   **6** M.C. Sexton, 'Who Invented Radio? – A Strange Controversy', *Studies*, 55 (1966) 415.

Figure 3.1 The transmitter developed at the Villa Griffone

Hertz in 1888 in some detail since it is *the* major milestone in the development of wireless communications. Hertz of Karlsruhe, student of Professor Helmholz (the first continental scientist to support Maxwell), not only demonstrated the existence of electro-magnetic waves but reflected, focussed and polarised them

Figure 3.2 The Marconi family with servants at the Villa Griffone photographed just before Marconi's departure for England with his mother. Guglielmo is standing on the right. His father Giuseppe is seated first right and his mother Annie is seated first left.

in precisely the same manner as could be done with light waves. He also demonstrated interference patterns to establish the wave character of the radiations, calculated the wave-lengths and finally measured their velocity as being identical with the velocity of light. His apparatus consisted of a radiating spark gap situated along the focal axis of a cylindrical parabolic mirror of sheet metal,[7] with the sparks being generated by an induction coil, in the primary circuit of which was a simple tapping key to make and break the circuit. The focussed rays were detected by observing the sparks from the induced oscillations jumping across the gap of a similar arrangement. The frequency of his oscillator was about five hundred megahertz per second, corresponding to a wavelength of sixty centimetres, and an extraordinary similarity exists between the focussing property of his equipment and that of modern radar and very high frequency (VHF) communications antennae.

It is not clear if Marconi attempted to repeat either the experiments of Hertz or the demonstration of Lodge, which would in all probability have been beyond his capability but, undaunted as usual, he decided to carry out his own practical tests:

7 This arrangement is quite similar to the working of a car headlamp.

> At my home near Bologna in Italy, I commenced early in 1895 to carry out tests and experiments with the object of determining whether it would be possible by means of Hertzian Waves to transmit to a distance telegraphic signs and symbols without the aid of connecting wires … After a few preliminary experiments with Hertzian Waves I became very soon convinced that if these waves or similar waves could be reliably transmitted and received over considerable distances a new system of communication would become available possessing enormous advantages over flashlights and optical methods, which are so much dependent for their success on the clearness of the atmosphere.[8]

Initially he began his tests in a large attic provided by his mother in the Villa Griffone and was soon transmitting dots and dashes throughout the house using conventional equipment (e.g. spark gap, induction coil, tapping keys and later, relays, bells, ink etc.) taken directly from the well-developed cable telegraph systems which had originated with the railways in the 1840s. He then moved outdoors and while working continuously on his signalling apparatus Marconi made a fundamental discovery:[9]

> In August 1895 I discovered a new arrangement which not only increased the distance over which I could communicate, but also seemed to make the transmission independent from the effects of intervening obstacles …
>
> This arrangement consisted in connecting one terminal of the Hertzian oscillation or spark-producer to earth and the other terminal to a wire or capacity area placed at a height above the ground, and in also connecting at the receiving end one terminal of the coherer to earth and the other to an elevated conductor. I then began to examine the relation between the distance at which the transmitter could affect the receiver and the elevation of the capacity areas above the earth, and I very soon definitely ascertained that the higher the wires or capacity areas, the greater the distance over which it was possible to telegraph.[10]

Marconi also found that the higher the wires or capacity areas, the greater the distance over which it was possible to telegraph. Furthermore the rearranged system seemed to make the transmission independent of the effects of inter-

8 Nobel lecture, op. cit. **9** This is the first of Marconi's three fundamental discoveries in electromagnetic wave propagation that revolutionized the world of communications in the twentieth century. The second was the 32-metre 'daylight' wave which inaugurated the short wave era in long-distance radio and the third was the over-the-horizon propagation of microwaves by tropospheric means which advanced the field of communications significantly, especially after the second world war: Bondyopadhay, 'Fleming and Marconi: cooperation of the century', *Radio Scientist* (URSI), 5/2, June 1994. **10** Nobel lecture, op. cit.

vening obstacles. This latter phenomenon was discovered when Marconi was able to receive signals on the far side of the hill near the Villa Griffone where his brother Alfonso fired a gun when the signal was received.[11]

Marconi's wireless propagation experiments in England
Marconi's mother Annie, who had stoutly encouraged Guglielmo and supported him financially, especially in 1894–5 at the Villa Griffone against the increasing opposition of his father, who felt that Marconi's antics were a complete waste of time ('*perdita completa di tempo*' as he remarked), now knew that there was far more than mere dilettante activity to her son's discoveries. She made every effort to advance his invention, but the first major attempt was rejected by the Italian Minister of Post and Telegraph. Nothing daunted, Annie decided to bring Marconi to England, the greatest maritime nation of the world at that time. Furthermore, she realised the great potential of his wireless invention in ship-to-shore and ship-to-ship communications, especially with maritime safety in mind. It is difficult for us to realise that only one hundred years ago a ship leaving port was completely on it own with no contact whatever with its departure harbour or anywhere else until it had again reached land which had a cable telegraph station.

Marconi and Annie left Bologna for London in January 1896 and by June of that year Marconi, with the assistance of his mother's Irish relations in London, filed for the world's first patent for wireless telegraphy (Radiation Wireless). The complete specifications were filed in March 1897. Marconi had some difficulty in having the patent accepted in England and, on his cousins' advice, had to engage some eminent scientific barristers to ensure success.

The major driving force behind Marconi in London proved to be his maternal cousin, Henry Jameson Davis, an engineer specialising in milling machinery, who arranged a meeting for Marconi with Sir William Preece, Chief Engineer of the all-powerful General Post Office. This meeting was successful and very soon, under the general aegis of the GPO, Marconi's demonstrations of his invention began in England.

> These experiments were continued in England, where in September 1896, a distance of 1¾ miles was obtained in tests carried out for the British Government on Salisbury Plain. The distance of communication was extended to 4 miles in March 1897 and in May of the same year to 9 miles.[12]

These tests will be referred to again in Chapter 6 when the work of one of Marconi's Irish engineers, Edwin Glanville, will be described.

---

11 G. Tabarroni, *Bologna e la Storia della Radiazione a 70 Anni dalla Prima Trasmissioni di G. Marconi a Villa Griffone* (Bologna: Tipografia Compositori, 1965). **12** Nobel lecture, op. cit.

Figure 3.3 Marconi's experiments on Salisbury Plain, 1896

The formation of Marconi's company

In order to further develop and commercialise his invention Marconi, acting on the advice of his cousin Jameson Davis, formed the Wireless Telegraph and Signal Company in July 1897 with a capital of £Stg100,000 [today, €6m]. The initial investments came from his mother, the Davis and Jameson relations and friends such as Saunders and Ballantynes with further money coming later from additional directors (see table A). Marconi received £15,000 [€900k] from his patents which paid for the initial formation of the Company and he himself received 60,000 of the 100,000 £1 shares with the remaining £40,000 put on the market for subscribers. £25,000 was provided as working capital. The share-holders/directors were Jameson Davis (Managing Director), Guglielmo Marconi (Technical Director), nine '*commercianti di ceriali*' i.e grain merchants, and one classified as 'A gentleman' and no known occupation for another. Most of the directors were Irish and from Dublin in particular. Edwin Glanville's comments on the directors are given in Chapter 6.

The immediate question to be asked is 'What exactly have grain merchants in common with a company at the frontier of electrical technology?' One expla-nation was that London, being the most important centre in the world for a cereals/grain market at that time, would benefit from the speed of the new system of wireless telegraphy, especially involving ships coming to England with their cargoes. However, in my opinion, it actually was a way of controlling the Company by Davis and Marconi since they were the only engineers on the Board, which really implied that the other shareholders, the grain merchants, had to rely on the professional advice and proposals for the Company by Davis and Marconi.

The fledgling company had difficulties from the beginning, largely because of opposition from the Post Office and its monopoly on telegraphy on British soil from the Telegraph Act of 1868. This forced Marconi to concentrate on communications involving both land and sea simultaneously. Besides, there were many technical problems to be solved before an up-and-running enterprise could be successful, and Marconi had already commenced building a factory at Chelmsford in Essex for his transmitters and receivers.

However, further inventions, improvements and experiments in signalling were not long in coming through Marconi's quite incredible energy and table B shows the extent of Marconi's successful research and testing on the English Channel between 1897 and 1899.

> After numerous tests and demonstrations over distances varying up to 40 miles, communication was established for the first time across the English Channel between England and France in March 1899.[13]

At this stage Marconi's ambitions were beginning to crystallise on a possible wireless connection with North America but he turned his attention to his mother's country of birth – Ireland – as his next logical step.

Table A *Names and professions of the persons who underwrote the Act of Establishment of the Wireless Telegraph Co., 20 July 1897*

James Fitgerald Ballantyne	Gentleman
Henry Jameson Davis	Engineer
Thomas Wiles	Grain Merchant
Henry Obré	Grain Merchant
M.T. Goodbody	Grain Merchant
Cyril F. Bennet	Grain Merchant
S.W. Ellerby	Grain Merchant
Robert A. Patterson	Unknown
Frank Wilson	Grain Merchant

---

13 Nobel lecture, op. cit.

Table B *Marconi's major achievements along the English Channel*

Alum Bay, Isle of Wight (Needles Hotel)	January 1898
Bournemouth on the Channel (Madeira House)	January 1898
Poole near Bournemouth, Dorset (Haven Hotel)	September 1898
Link between South Foreland Lighthouse near Dover on the Channel with the lightship of East Goodwin	Winter 1898
Temporary station at South Foreland for transmission across the Channel to Wimereaux, near Boulogne	Spring 1899

CHAPTER 4

Marconi arrives in Ireland

Ballycastle – Rathlin Island Wireless Link, Co. Antrim

Having made a profound impression in the English scene with the wireless tests over land, ship-to-shore and ship-to-ship, Marconi had his first commercial break which, strangely enough, also led him to his first visit to Ireland. Geographically, Ireland was almost central to the Northern Europe–North America shipping routes and equally – or more importantly – raised the distinct possibility of establishing a direct viable wireless link between the two continents on account of their relative close proximity.

Since 1858 there had been intermittent cable telegraphic connections between North America and Europe via Ireland, with the Irish station located on Valentia Island, just off the South Kerry coast. It was only in 1866 that a long-lasting cable was finally laid with Lord Kelvin (William Thomson from Belfast) as chief engineer of the project.

The commercial break came from Lloyds of London which already had a semaphore station located at Torr Head in the north-east corner of County Antrim from which they reported ships passing through the North Channel between Ireland and Scotland. Frequently, however, in conditions of bad visibility, contact with ships could not be established. Although many of these ships passed very close to Rathlin Island and made contact with the lighthouse there was no means of conveying this information to Torr Head. Lloyds requested the Marconi Company to establish a wireless link between Rathlin Island and Ballycastle on the mainland to overcome this obstacle.

The most outlying places can, from time to time, be linked with the great names of the world; Rathlin Island – a hilly fragment of land, five miles long, one quarter-mile wide maximum, and only four miles from the North Antrim coast, is specifically referred to by the Latin scholar Pliny as an island between Ireland and Britain, and the Egyptian philosopher Ptolemy in the second century AD also refers to Rathlin in his geographical studies. It is quite astonishing that the island was known to Pliny and Ptolemy almost two thousand years before it again flickered into prominence in connection with the early development of wireless telegraphy.[1]

---

[1] H.A. Boyd, *Marconi and Ballycastle*, Co. Antrim Library, ref. U/A BLA 1274477. August 1968.

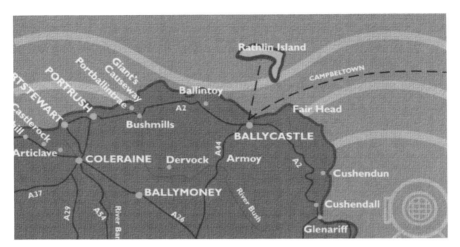

Figure 4.1 The north-east of Ireland showing the Ballycastle–Rathlin Ireland wireless link

Marconi himself was fully occupied with his experiments in England and entrusted the setting up to George Kemp, Post Office technician, ex-Royal Navy, and released by the chief engineer of the British Post Office, William Preece, to work with Marconi and later with Edwin Glanville, graduate of Trinity College, Dublin with first-class honours in Mathematics and Experimental Science. Actually Marconi was delighted with this connection with Lloyds (his first commercial contract) which provided urgently needed finance.

It was decided that the signals should come from the East lighthouse of Rathlin Island, where Glanville was put in charge, to a receiving station in Ballycastle where they would be decoded and relayed on to Lloyds' station at Torr Head by telephone. The spark transmitter and batteries were installed in the lighthouse and an almost vertical aerial wire initially eighty feet high and later extended to one hundred feet was attached from the top of the lighthouse to the rocks beneath and appropriately insulated.

However, finding a suitable location in Ballycastle, 7½ miles across land and sea from the transmitter/receiver proved to be a far more difficult affair. The first attempt using the flagstaff on Ballycastle pier, although directly opposite Rathlin, was a complete failure. On 6 July 1898 the first test signals were received from Rathlin, by Kemp at the 'Weightmasters Cottage' of the Ballycastle coalmines near Carrigmore, Fair Head. These were sent by lightkeeper Dunovan from the East light. In his meticulously-kept daily diary, Kemp called his location the 'coal store' and described the aerial leading over the road to a small mast at the top of the cliff behind the cottage. In early July, Glanville had not yet arrived and Kemp had not received the spars, masts and insulators for other potential sites. This cottage, which still exists, is the closest mainland building to the East Light with

Figure 4.2 Aerial photograph of Rathlin Island facing north showing the east lighthouse where Marconi's wireless apparatus was located. Ballycastle is approximately 4½ miles to the south.

Figure 4.3 The east lighthouse at the top of the sheer cliff face

Figure 4.4 Mr Ernest Shannon, present owner of White Lodge House, with the author. The plaque commemorates Marconi's first transmission to the island in July 1898

a transmission path entirely over sea which was much favoured by Marconi. It was a natural site for a first test but the lack of a telegraph or telephone line was a serious disadvantage for a permanent station and there was no guarantee that the station would be permanent – correctly as it transpired. The building is still called 'Marconi's Cottage' to this day although some doubt exists as to whether Kemp ever actually used the cottage.[2] Actually, the first reasonably reliable signal was received at the White Lodge House.

The Preece method of an electromagnetic induction link between Ballycastle and Rathlin Island – competition with Marconi

In 1884 William Preece discovered that messages sent through insulated wires buried in iron pipes in the streets of London were inadvertently picked up on telephone circuits erected on poles above the housetops eighty feet away. Ordinary telephone circuits were found to produce disturbances and even distinct telephone speech was subsequently detected up to 1.25 miles. By 1887 enough information was available to confirm that these effects were due to electromagnetic waves entirely free from any earth conduction.

Preece realised that this electromagnetic 'nuisance' might be used to advantage in certain limited situations over existing telephone and telegraph lines, but only where the lengths of the overhead transmitting and receiving coils (completed by earth conduction) were comparable with the distance between them. Accordingly, the only situation where the induction system might be advantageous would be for communicating several miles across an estuary or with a nearby offshore island.

2 P. Clarke, 'Marconi in Ballycastle / Rathlin Island', Lecture to Ballycastle Community Association, October 1983.

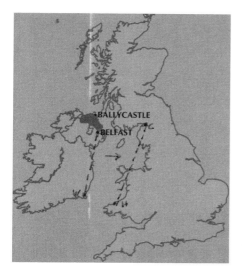

Figure 4.5 Location of Preece's effort to establish an inductive transmission between Ireland and England by linking telephone wires to form gigantic current loops with an earth return in the two islands (see p. 38)

In his first test in 1892 across the Bristol Channel near Cardiff, Preece established two parallel circuits between the riverbank and two islands in the estuary over a maximum distance of 3.3 miles. Each circuit became successively the primary and secondary of an induction system according to the direction in which the signals were being sent. The alternator 'gave smooth sinusoidal curves with 260 vibrations per second to give a pleasant note to the ear, easily read when broken up by the key into dots and dashes'. Preece subsequently repeated this test involving some lighthouses and islands around the coast which (although he did not admit it) were almost total failures.

The 1897 paper by Preece shows Marconi's tests over the same path in the Bristol Channel. He describes Marconi's apparatus fully, noting, in an almost fulsome manner, that Marconi had succeeded in transmitting across the entire channel of almost nine miles, a fact that Preece had signally failed to accomplish. This paper is reproduced in full in Appendix 3.[3]

A curious fact is that five years elapsed between the actual tests (Preece 1892, Marconi 1897), although this is not immediately clear from Preece's paper and an account of the Marconi experiment in 1897, recalled in 1962 by his eldest daughter Degna, makes no reference whatever to Preece's work.[4]

Notwithstanding his indifferent results with the induction and – far more importantly – the fundamental range limitation, Preece set about attempting to send signals by induction across the Irish Sea.[5] In June 1895 he had a continuous section of the overhead telegraph system in Ireland connected in series from

3 W.G. Preece, 'Signalling through space without wires', *The Electrician*, 11 June 1897.   4 D. Marconi, *My Father Marconi*.   5 P. Clarke, 'Marconi's Irish connections recalled', *100 Years of Radio*, IEE Conference Publication No. 411, September 1995.

Belfast to Wexford facing a similar connection from Carlisle in north-west England to Haverford West in South Wales. These connections were hundreds of miles long (comparable with the varying distances between the opposing coasts) but no recognisable signal whatever was received in England when the Irish line was activated. Presumably both lines had been checked for continuity with return earth – they constituted in effect a gigantic transformer, but even Preece realised that the distances were well outside the scope of his system and the sheer impracticability of the test itself was mind-boggling and, not for the first time, his credibility took a knock. Previously he had come off worst in a famous debate with Oliver Lodge (the inventor of the syntonic or tuned circuit) regarding the electrical mechanisms in play on lightning arresters attached to telegraph poles. Preece had claimed *total* expertise since the British Post Office had erected half a million poles under his direction. Lodge replied by stating acidly that *one* pole was sufficient for the research. In fact Preece, who appears to have been a bluff, aggressive character, was hopelessly out of his depth in dealing with electromagnetic giants such as Maxwell, Fitzgerald, Hertz, Heaviside et al.

CHAPTER 5

Kingstown Regatta and the royal sequel

The summer yachting regattas around the coasts of Britain were extremely popular sporting events at the turn of the twentieth century. Large yachts with foreign royalty and wealthy businessmen such as Sir Thomas Lipton moved around the coasts like a travelling circus competing with each other, to the great enjoyment of the inhabitants of each town who were eager to get a glimpse of the 'glitterati' and ponder on the social affairs of the yacht owners, some of whom had large steam cruising vessels.

The Royal St George Yacht Club in Kingstown (now Dún Laoghaire) was due to hold its annual regatta in late July 1898 and the Dublin *Daily Express* and its sister paper *Evening Mail* decided to commemorate the centenary of the latter by reporting the yachting results by wireless – the very first of its kind. Marconi, always alert to publicity, readily acceded to a request to transmit reports by wireless telegraph from the high seas and on 6 July 1898 ordered Kemp and Glanville to bring the wireless equipment from Ballycastle to Kingstown. This was the same day that Kemp had received his first satisfactory signal from Rathlin. Lloyds had no objection to this diversion since they saw the financial advantage of setting up marine communications. There were eyebrows raised in some quarters amongst those who saw the new invention as an instrument for serious lifesaving and business and military messages but the Dublin newspapers were determined to initiate the use of wireless telegraphy applied to journalism and this would be the very first reporting of a sporting event.

Initially George Kemp was very concerned about moving his equipment, even temporarily, from Ballycastle to Kingstown but he was reassured, almost certainly by Edwin Glanville, that most of the requirements including the spark induction coil made by Nicholas Callan were already in Professor Fitzgerald's laboratory in Trinity College, Dublin, the only vital element missing being the sensitive coherer designed and fabricated by Marconi himself.

Marconi hired a tugboat called the *Flying Huntress* to monitor the yacht races about 7–9 miles out in Dublin Bay and installed his land station in the Harbour Master's Office in Kingstown. The following extracts are taken directly from the primary source, the *Evening Mail* of 21 July 1898, and the article by Professor

G.F. Fitzgerald on the meaning and possibilities of the new phenomenon is reproduced in full in Appendix 1.

Wireless Telegraphy Applied to Journalism
The Experiment Explained.
On Board the Flying Huntress
By an Unscientific Observer

The *Flying Huntress*, though a creditable craft, was obviously not built for beauty, and with Signor Marconi's magic netting hanging from an impromptu mast she looked somewhat bizarre. I stepped on board with an anxious sense of the disproportion between the wonderful character of the discovery which was about to be put in practical operation and the apparently prosaic character of the means taken to wrest Nature's secrets from her. Still there was something humorously congruous in the title of the tug, for not even the fleet-footed Atalanta – the swiftest creation of Greek fancy – could catch one of our up-to-date 'sparks' when the latter are sent on their way by the enchanter's touch of Signor Marconi. In the small cabin of the tug there was not much to strike the casual observer. A transmitter, a receiver, an ordinary Morse taping-machine, and two batteries underneath the plain wooden table. The instruments were connected with the outer world by a copper wire, which was itself attached to a width of wire-netting – ordinary rabbit-netting it was – which ran up to the top of the improvised mast, and in its meshes caught millions of the myriad electric waves which (when replies were coming) were generated at the land station and sent down to us here in the modest cabin of an unassuming tug-boat nine miles off shore. The wonder of it. The deck of a steamer was wont to be considered the ideal spot for 'dolce far niente' – no post, no newspapers, no chatter of the madding crowd. A splendid isolation indeed … As Signor Marconi stepped in to the cabin it was impossible to check exclamations of surprise at his youthful appearance. A tall, athletic figure, dark hair, steady grey blue eyes, a resolute mouth, and an open forehead – such is the young Italian inventor. His manner is at once unassuming to a degree, and yet confident. He speaks freely and fully, and quite frankly defines the limits of his own as of all scientists' knowledge as to the mysterious powers of electricity and ether. At his instrument his face shows a suppressed enthusiasm which is a delightful revelation of character. A youth of twenty-three who can, very literally, evoke spirits from the vasty deep and despatch them on the wings of the wind must naturally feel that he has done something very like picking the lock of Nature's laboratory. Signor Marconi listens to the crack-crack of his instrument with some such wondering interest as

Aladdin must have displayed on first hearing the voice of the Genius who had been called up by the friction of his lamp. For my part, as I looked at the boyish figure of the operator as he flashed news over nine miles of sea I felt that I had been privileged to assist at an experiment that was destined to revolutionise our means of communication and link nation to nation by the strong yet subtle bonds of the 'viewless winds'. Prospero's Island with its spirits, will henceforth be a true image of the world. To quote the eloquent peroration of a lecture by Professor Lodge delivered at the Royal Institution: 'The present is an epoch of astounding activity in physical science. Progress is a thing of months and weeks, almost of days. The long lines of isolated ripples of past discovery seem blending into a mighty wave, on the crest of which one begins to discern some oncoming magnificent generalisation. The suspense is becoming feverish, at times almost painful. One feels like a boy, who has been long strumming on the silent keyboard of a deserted organ, into the chest of which an unseen power begins to blow a vivifying breath. Astonished, he now finds that the touch of a finger elicits a responsive note, and he hesitates, half-delighted, half-affrighted, lest he be deafened by the chords which it seems he can now summon almost at his will'.

At the Land Station.
With Signor Marconi's Chief Assistant.

In a room at the rear of the residence of the Harbourmaster there were duplicates of the instruments on the steamer. A wire from these was carried in a vertical line to the top of a mast forty feet in height, which has been erected for the purpose of these experiments on the hill behind, and on which is a similar wire netting arrangement to that which is attached to the mast of the steamer. The receiver, the transmitter, and Morse tape-machine occupy a small table about four feet square. In the little room were Mr. Kemp (Signor Marconi's chief assistant), Mr. Glanville, a graduate of Trinity and a pupil of the Professor Fitzgerald, with the present writer and another member of the *Daily Express* staff. While the tug was forging her way to the Kish lightship the final preparations were made for receiving and transmitting messages.[1]

During the two-day event more than 700 reports of the various racing competitions were successfully transmitted by Marconi, printed out on shore on a Morse Tape machine, decoded and forwarded by telephone to the Dublin newspapers

---

1 *Dublin Evening Mail*, 21 July 1898.

Figure 5.1 Marconi in 1898

for publication. Indeed, some were posted up on the windows of the newspaper offices to the mixture of delight or chagrin of the betting fraternity. The experiment had been a spectacular success both from a journalistic and commercial aspect and established Marconi as the leading figure in this new and rapidly expanding field of commercial communications.

Return to Ballycastle
Immediately after the races, Marconi returned to England with his special assistant Bullock. Kemp, along with Granville, set out for Ballycastle/Rathlin to continue the Lloyds shipping contract, with Glanville transmitting from Rathlin to enable Kemp to locate the best receiving site on the mainland. Initially the most successful involved the suspension of the aerial from the spire of the local Catholic church, courtesy of the parish priest, but understandably enough Lloyds were not over enthusiastic about this arrangement in North Antrim. The important point was that adequate signals could be received in Ballycastle itself. In early August a room was taken in a cliff-top house, (the 'White Lodge', now 'Glenmara') which had a clear view of the whole island and received an erratic reception. To Kemp's shock though, a message received on 21 August reported the accidental death of Glanville, who had fallen 300ft off a sheer cliff on Rathlin.

The first commercial messages for Lloyds were sent on 20 August, reporting the names of ten ships passing Rathlin East Lighthouse in a fog that would have made it impossible ever to locate them from Torr Head. Further messages were sent in the following days and clearly represented the breakthrough to the commercial world which Marconi badly needed. It must not be forgotten that

Figure 5.2 The *Flying Huntress* showing apparatus for 'catching' electric waves.
It was actually rabbit wire.

the Marconi Company had been launched by raising £100,000 two years previously.

Marconi himself finally arrived in Ballycastle on 29 August, just in time for the 'Ould Lammas Fair'. He would have come much sooner but for a peremptory *Diktat* from Queen Victoria to set up a wireless link between the Isle of Wight and the royal yacht *Osborne* at Cowes. He was in a state of considerable grief arising from Glanville's untimely death. In fact, he was so upset that, apart from working with Kemp on the wireless installation, he passed most of his time alone in his room at the Antrim Arms Hotel in Ballycastle. The fact that Marconi and Glanville were both in their early twenties must have compounded his depression.

During his five days in Ballycastle, Marconi actually attended the Lammas Fair, examined the various experimental sites and visited Fair Head, Torr Head and, of course, Rathlin. Contemporary accounts indicate that he visited the cliff face from which Glanville had fallen to his untimely death.

The successful demonstrations were not immediately followed up by a permanent installation for Lloyds by Marconi, mainly because the British Post Office was now claiming the monopoly on *all* communications under the Telegraph Act of 1868, which gave the Postmaster-General power to acquire, work and maintain telegraph installations on land *and within territorial waters.*

Figure 5.3 Marconi transmitting a wireless despatch from the cabin of the *Daily Express* steamer.
Professor George Fitzgerald from Trinity College, Dublin is wearing the cape (2nd
from left) and Professor Gerald Molloy from the Royal University (now University College,
Dublin) is wearing the cap (3rd from left). The Callan induction coil operated by Marconi
is described in Appendix 2.

Deregulation was clearly not an option for some time yet. The influence of
Preece may be detected in this since, although initially welcoming Marconi on
his arrival from Italy in 1896 with every assistance, including the secondment of
Kemp, who subsequently spent the remainder of his working life in the service
of Marconi (he died in 1933), now saw Marconi as a potentially independent
competitor in the newly emerging wireless telegraphy. Moreover, Marconi was
concentrating on ship-to-ship and ship-to-shore wireless (mainly lighthouses)
for safety reasons at sea. Accordingly his equipment was moving in and out of
territorial waters to Preece's chagrin. He also had influential friends in London
through his mother and his cousin Henry Jameson Davis.

From July to September 1898, the wireless link using aerials, developed by
Marconi, was operated very satisfactorily by Kemp and Glanville until the latter's
tragic death in August. Then, out of the blue, Preece ordered the complete
closedown of Marconi's system, much to the annoyance of Lloyds, and replaced
it with his induction circuitry similar to his partially successful 3.3 mile transmission across the Bristol Channel (see Appendix 3). The path chosen was 3.5
miles between Rue Point near the East lighthouse on Rathlin where he had to
spread out the line for the distance involved, facing a three-mile stretch of
telegraph wire on the mainland from Fair Head to within one mile of Ballycastle

(he had previously carried out the same tests across Murlough Bay near Fair Head). It is almost certain that this wire ran directly over 'Marconi's Cottage' which was not used by Preece for his transmissions, who moved his equipment to Ballycastle Post Office. The link lasted from 1901 to 1906, by which time the superiority of Marconi's radiation method was established beyond question. As far as can be ascertained the Morse code was only replaced by a radio telephone in 1935.

It must be emphasised that Preece's induction system *was* a success at Ballycastle and wireless signals using both Morse code and even speech telephony were sent and received. It was the only reasonably satisfactory long distance link (3.5 miles) of Sir William Preece's Induction System which was put to commercial use. It was a most cumbersome and unwieldy system and hardly justified the complete closedown of both Irish and English telegraph networks for about 12 hours to cater for the pet project of the Engineer-in-Chief.

In retrospect, Preece may also have had a lingering personal annoyance against Marconi over an event which had occurred some time previously in Alum Bay, Isle of Wight where Marconi had set up an experimental station to examine transmissions over water. In June 1898, two distinguished visitors, Lords Kelvin and Tennyson, accompanied by their wives, were invited by Marconi to view his wireless experiments at Alum Bay. Having previously and disparagingly described 'wireless telegraphy' as being no better than 'a boy on a pony', Kelvin was now so impressed that with Marconi's approval he not only sent wireless telegrams to some colleagues including Preece, but also insisted on paying one shilling for each one. One of Kelvin's telegrams reads:

> To Maclean, Physical laboratory, University, Glasgow Tell Blyth that this is transmitted commercially through ether [*sic*] from Alum Bay to Bournemouth and by postal telegraph thence to Glasgow. Kelvin.

Tennyson telegraphed his nephew at Cambridge in similar tones ending with: '*Very sorry not to hear you speak your Thackeray tomorrow*'.[2]

Both Marconi and Kelvin realised perfectly well that, by the payment for the telegrams, they were challenging the GPO monopoly which, of course, did not go unnoticed by Preece.

The royal sequel: Marconi meets Queen Victoria
The spectacular success of the wireless transmissions announcing the results of the Kingstown Regatta were, of course, immediately published by the Dublin newspapers and the London *Times* and attracted the attention of Queen Victoria,

2 D. Marconi, *My Father Marconi.*

now approaching eighty, who was in residence in the Isle of Wight at Osborne House. Her son and heir, the Prince of Wales, had recently injured his knee in a fall down the stairs at the Rothschild palace in Paris and he was not particularly keen on spending his period of partial personal immobility at his mother's house. He preferred to pass the time aboard the royal yacht which was moored in Cowes Bay approximately two miles away, out of sight of Osborne House. Here the fifty-seven-year-old Prince, who did not accede to the throne until the death of his mother in 1901, could lead an independent social life with visits from nearby friends and officers of the Royal Navy, stationed nearby for Cowes Week.

Marconi was asked to provide a wireless installation so that the Queen could communicate with the royal yacht even when it had slipped its moorings for a brief trip. The possibility of the future king hobbling around indefinitely on crutches or at the very least with a walking stick was a horrifying prospect to her, and relations between the Queen and Prince were strained enough without this additional factor.

The whole project almost came to an abrupt and untimely end when Marconi, who was installing the wireless system in a cottage in the grounds of Osborne House, was curtly told by a gardener to 'go back and round' as the Queen was 'out *walking* in her Bath-Chair' and would strongly resent any intrusion on her privacy. Marconi refused point-blank to alter his route and the matter was immediately reported to the Queen whose royal comment was 'Get me another electrician'. She was ultimately forced to relent when told diplomatically that there *was* no other electrician in England to replace Marconi. In fact she subsequently granted Marconi an audience to congratulate him on the success of the wireless link.

Marconi's comment to an assemblage of engineers about the link was that he had accepted the invitation 'with true pleasure for it offered me the opportunity to study and meditate upon new and interesting elements concerning the influence of hills on wireless communication'. His preparations were even more scrupulous than ever for this particular test. A vertical conductor was attached to the main mast of the Royal Yacht at a height of 83ft above the deck and a coil capable of producing a 10-inch spark was used. The land station in the grounds of Osborne House had a 100ft high antenna.

In the sixteen days that followed, 150 messages crossed the hills and the water between the house and the ship, many of them as long as 150 words, at an average rate of 15 words per minute. The Prince of Wales gave permission to Marconi to reveal the bulletins about his health. On 4 August his private physician Sir James Real wirelessed to her Majesty: '*HRH the Prince of Wales has passed another excellent night and is in very good spirits and health. The knee is most satisfactory.*' And on the 5th: '*HRH the Prince of Wales has passed another excellent night and the knee is in good condition.*' Note that the second message is not *quite* as positive as the first. Was there an indirect hint to Her Majesty that all was not completely well?

These wireless telegrams were actually reproduced in Marconi's seminal paper in the *Journal of the Institution of Electrical Engineers*, following his lecture to the IEE in March 1899.[3] It was his first public discourse in English and he displayed remarkable composure in answering questions before an audience which included some of the most distinguished 'electricians' of the time, J.A. Fleming, S.P. Thomson, and A.C. Campbell Swinton.[4]

So delighted were the members of the royal family that they continued their communications during the Cowes Regatta. Various royal dukes and duchesses, even cabinet ministers, joined in issuing invitations to tea, aperitifs, dinner etc. in what was in effect a prelude to the age of radio hams.

For his part, Marconi took full advantage of the yacht voyages around Cowes, not only to study the effects of the intervening hills on the transmission but also to verify reliable contacts between lighthouses and lightships with the shore and other ships. It was Marconi's desire that the men on lonely lightships and isolated lighthouses should be able also to 'send daily messages of a private character to render less painful their isolation'.

During the question-and-answer session following Marconi's paper, Marconi was specifically asked about the possibility of using the Fastnet Rock Lighthouse off the south-west coast of Ireland for transmissions/receptions. This would seem to indicate clearly that he was already laying the groundwork for his next major commercial venture to set up a wireless station near Crookhaven Co. Cork.

The arrival of tuned (syntonic) circuits

As a final remark concerning wireless telegraphy in those very early days, the question may well be asked, 'how would these primitive systems have performed if tuned, originally called 'syntonic', circuits had been available?' As it happened, Oliver Lodge had already in 1890 demonstrated and patented 'syntonic circuits' using Leyden jars as capacitors and what we would now describe as twin-wire transmission lines tuned or syntonised by movable short circuits.[5] However, the full implications of tuning were only realised by Marconi when the proliferation of wireless transmitters literally clogged the airwaves indiscriminately making correct identification of transmitters virtually impossible – a serious matter for

---

3 G. Marconi, 'Wireless Telegraphy', *Journal of the Institution of Electrical Engineers*, 28 (1899), 273.
4 Silvanus Thomson in particular appears to have been a sharp-tongued individual whose classic text entitled 'Calculus Made Easy' is prefaced by the old Simeon proverb 'What one fool can do, another can'. Many years ago the school physics master of the present writer commented 'But Silvanus Thomson was no fool'. 5 O.J. Lodge, *Receiver in Syntonic Jar Experiment, Signalling across Space without Wires: The Work of Hertz and his Successors*, (London: Electrician Printing and Publishing Co., 1894).

marine communications in particular. The Marconi Company was forced to buy out Lodge's patent at the huge cost of £20,000 (today €1m) as well as employing Lodge as a consultant for several years. This would appear to be one of the few, if not the only, major commercial setback during Marconi's meteoric rise to international acclaim, but it nearly bankrupted the fledgling company.

CHAPTER 6

Edwin Glanville, unsung hero of wireless telegraphy

In the preceding chapter we noted the significant work of Edwin Glanville regarding the Ballycastle-Rathlin wireless link which Kemp and himself perfected for the Lloyds' contract. He also introduced the Morse code both to the lighthouse keepers and to the Lloyds agent on the island. Furthermore, his professional knowledge of the then emerging 'signals without wires', arising from his university education in TCD under the tutelage of Professor G.F. Fitzgerald, was undoubtedly a significant factor in the success of reporting the results of the Kingstown Regatta in July 1898.[1] Marconi's technical assistants must, of course, be given full credit for this also in this sensational transmission over sea – a test which had huge implications for marine safety.

However, Glanville's role in Marconi's first involvements in Ireland at Ballycastle and Kingstown seems to have all but faded into obscurity, unlike that of George Kemp whose name is indelibly associated with those two exciting events and with others yet to come. The major difference is, of course, that whereas Kemp became Marconi's permanent personal assistant and lived until 1933, only four years before Marconi's death in 1937, Glanville's employment lasted only eighteen months. It should be mentioned that the value of Glanville's work has been referred to occasionally over the past 100 years but a proper recognition of his achievements is long overdue. Very recently I have been given access by the Glanville family in Dublin to hitherto unpublished correspondence from Glanville to his family over the period 1897–8. The true worth of his work for the Marconi Company is quite clear from these letters. The most significant information from the letters is that, contrary to the usual assertion, Glanville actually *preceded* Kemp in employment by the Marconi Company.

Edward Edwin Glanville was born in Dublin in 1873, eldest son of Edward Samuel Glanville and Jane Price. He had two sisters, and one brother who died at the age of nine from scarlet fever. The Glanville family had originally come from Moate, Co. Westmeath, and Edwin's father was owner of a Marble Works

---

1 *Dublin Evening Mail* (Supplement), 21 July 1898.

who designed and fabricated the marble staircase in the Venetian-style Engineering Building in Trinity College, Dublin (TCD). It should be noted that amongst the family the young Glanville was usually called 'Edwin'.

Following school education at Wesley College, Dublin, Edwin entered TCD in June 1891 and read for a degree in Mathematics and Experimental Science, gaining the overall 1st Class Degree of BA in 1895. In his final year, 1894–5, he had been awarded a Foundation Scholarship in Science, obtaining second place out of eight applicants and was formally conferred in 1896. Subsequently he undertook some postgraduate studies for which he successfully sat his final examination in April 1898.

In July 1897 he joined the Wireless Telegraph and Signal Co. (later changed to the Marconi Wireless Telegraph Co.) as a professional 'electrician' which was the name given to electrical engineers at the time. The exact manner in which he became an employee seems to be somewhat vague but it is certain that his tutor, Professor Fitzgerald, was very well known in what was then the tiny field of wireless, and corresponded frequently with Heinrich Hertz, especially after the latter's epoch-making experiment in 1888. Some of this correspondence is currently in the Deutsche Museum in Munich. Furthermore Glanville himself, in all probability would have read Sir Oliver Lodge's Commemoration Lecture on Hertz published in *The Electrician* in 1894,[2] and, more importantly, an account of Marconi's spectacular wireless demonstration over several kilometres on Salisbury Plain in September 1896 before an assembly of top military brass and senior GPO engineers. Marconi himself would have been favourably disposed towards Glanville as, apart from his excellent degree, both theoretical and practical, his background was firmly Dublin Irish for several generations and as the correspondence shows, Marconi was already considering expanding his activities to Ireland. In addition they were both close in age.

Following an initial period in London, Edwin Glanville was sent by Marconi to Salisbury Plain where ongoing further trials were carried out following the initial success. These Salisbury Plain tests involved the gathering of information mainly about the efficiency of various aerials and their ability to concentrate the wireless beams in a preferred direction. The refinement of this work was absolutely vital for the Clifden transatlantic station.

In the letter dated 12 October 1897 to his stepmother from his accommodation in Salisbury, Edwin wrote that three Marconi staff including himself had come down to 'make some experiments that Mr Marconi is trying. The transmitting instruments were in a GPO tent on top of a hill and receiver was in what they call a cart here but it was more like a kind of covered wagonette. We use flags for signalling purposes.'[3] The Army, Navy and GPO engineers were

2 O.J. Lodge, 'The work of Hertz', *The Electrician*, vol. 33 (1894). 3 Correspondence from Edwin

present for most of the time and Edwin wrote that 'we have a Royal Engineer to help. The Royal Engineers look after all the telegraph lines in the South of England'. I think that their presence was mainly to find out exactly what the Marconi Company was doing and report back to their superiors. As it turned out relations between Marconi and the GPO in particular were not long to remain friendly and mutual mistrust, if not hostility, was never far from the surface. In fact when Sir Alexander Fleming was appointed consultant to the Company, one of the first comments that he made was 'The less you have to do with the GPO the better.'

The letter of 12 October was the one in which Marconi informed Edwin Glanville about his forthcoming visit to Ireland after he had given an exhibition in Scotland. Edwin also wrote a revealing comment about Marconi to his stepmother: 'He is very nice but a bit shy and nervous'. It may have been that Marconi was slightly (but only slightly) in awe of Edwin with his first-class academic qualifications compared with Marconi's somewhat self-taught, erratic education in Italy, especially relating to electromagnetics.

Edwin's letter of 21 November 1897 from London was very informative regarding the directors and shareholders of the Company. He was a shareholder himself and accordingly entitled to attend meetings. At this particular meeting, some days before Edwin wrote the letter, Marconi announced that he had succeeded in signalling between Salisbury and Bath, a distance of thirty-four miles. This had been achieved before Edwin arrived in Salisbury but had been kept secret until the shareholders' meeting, obviously to impress the attendance. After the meeting many of the directors and shareholders were taken to see the equipment in working order and as Edwin remarked rather acidly in the letter: 'They asked idiotic questions etc.' Many of the directors were, in fact, from Dublin and included Mr Robert Goodbody who, according to Edwin 'did not ask stupid questions, observed the operations, taking a genuine interest in everything'.

One extremely significant comment in the letter was the remark by Edwin that the company had taken on 'a new man named Kemp ... He is a good practical man who has been in the Post Office factory. He is an old fellow, I should think about 45'. In fact George Kemp was released on loan to Marconi by Sir William Preece, Chief Engineer of the Post Office and actually was Marconi's personal assistant until his death in 1933. The interesting and revealing fact is that, as mentioned previously, Kemp was generally thought to have *preceded* Edwin Glanville in employment with the Company and accordingly, would possibly have been Edwin Glanville's immediate 'de facto' superior,

Glanville to his family, 1898 (courtesy of the Glanville family). The author is deeply appreciative of the generosity of Mrs Jane Glanville and Mr Patrick Glanville (who is a nephew of Edwin) in providing the hitherto unknown letters from Edwin to his stepmother together with newspaper extracts etc. relating to the tragedy in Rathlin.

especially in view of his age but bearing in mind his status as technician, although an excellent one, Kemp would hardly have been in a position to officially direct Edwin Glanville, except in an advisory capacity. Furthermore the phrase 'a good practical man', used by Edwin, is usually university-speak even today to describe someone who is excellent in the laboratory but deficient in something else such as theory. This may well have fitted Kemp's personality since when discussing the great achievement at Kingstown Regatta with the Press he referred to professors now having to burn their books and produce another theory to explain the true nature of signals without wires.

In a lighter vein in this letter, Edwin Glanville, when referring to the hordes of cyclists passing along a road near to his lodgings in London on a Sunday, told his stepmother that 'Annie' (his younger sister) 'will be pleased to know that a good many of the ladies don't wear skirts'. The next two letters from Edwin Glanville were from the Royal Needles Hotel, Alum Bay, Isle of Wight dated 14 January and 20 February 1898 . This indicates that his stay there was at least two months, but almost certainly much longer. The uncertainty arises since no further correspondence from Edwin has been discovered until his arrival in Ballycastle Co. Antrim in July 1898, but, in my opinion, it is reasonable to assume that he remained in Marconi's employment during all this time working along the English side of the Channel.

The Needles Hotel at Alum Bay was the first of several permanent wireless stations set up as bases for continuous trials as public demonstrations. A second station was set up in the Madeira Hotel, Bournemouth, referred to in Edwin's letter of 14 January, later transferred to the Haven Hotel, Poole, Dorset where it remained until 1926 (correspondence between the Haven Hotel and Crookhaven still exists). The stations were all similar, with the converted hotel rooms containing the transmitting and receiving apparatus, a few laboratory instruments for experimental work and very simple workshop facilities. From Poole and Alum Bay Marconi carried out extensive tests over land and sea involving lightships and light houses and also a small hired ship in which he nearly drowned on one occasion in a stormy sea with two feet of water in the wireless cabin. There is little doubt about Edwin Glanville's participation in these wireless tests which actually culminated in a successful cross-channel link between Dover and Wimereoux in 1899. This was a major achievement.

Edwin Glanville displayed flashes of humour – or perhaps dry wit – in the letters to his family. In his letter of 14 January 1898 he recalls that 'the owner of the Royal Needles Hotel Mr Millar was very fond of billiards. Mr Bullock [another Marconi assistant who later went to Kingstown] also plays very well but Mr Marconi's play is wonderful. His theory is that if you hit hard enough you are sure to get something, it doesn't always come off however!'

Glanville was also familiar with the electromagnetic interests of Professor

Figure 6.1 Edward Edwin Glanville (1873–98)

Molloy of the Royal University (now the National University of Ireland at University College Dublin) as he refers in his letter of 20 February 1898 from Alum Bay to a forthcoming lecture to be given by Professor Molloy on 16 March for which Dr Trouton of TCD would be assisting him with some instruments on loan from Marconi. It will be recalled that Professor Molloy was on board the *Flying Huntress* at the Kingstown Regatta accompanying Marconi and Fitzgerald.

Finally Glanville and Kemp arrived in Ballycastle on 25 July 1898 from Dublin by train immediately after the Kingstown Regatta and stayed at the Antrim Arms Hotel as noted in his letter of that date. Kemp was returning to Ballycastle to continue the setting up of the wireless link with Rathlin Island. Edwin Glanville was fully aware of the historic transmission of 6 July and went immediately to Rathlin where he was in charge of the new wireless station near the East light-house with Kemp located on the mainland at Ballycastle. His last contact with his family was in the form of a postcard from Rathlin Island itself on 4 August 1898 in which he wondered 'what had become of Mr Marconi who had gone to London after leaving Kingstown intending to come here in a few days'. We now know that he had been summoned by the Queen to monitor her son's social behaviour on the royal yacht.

Glanville was instructed to transmit every day and, in this manner, Kemp checked out the church steeple and the White Lodge cliff top house for receiving suitability, as already mentioned. Glanville would also, almost certainly, have introduced the Lloyds agent on the island, Mr Byrne, as well as the lighthouse-keeper Mr Dunovan and sons to the Morse code and general explanations of the spark gap transmitter and coherer-type receiver.[4]

Then, on Sunday, 21 August, tragedy struck when, out for a walk on that

---

4 P. Clarke, 'Marconi in Ballycastle / Rathlin Island'.

afternoon, Edwin Glanville apparently slipped on a cliff and fell 300ft to his death. This sad accident was quite unconnected with the wireless experiments and the island people had previously seen him climbing over the cliffs pursuing his interest in geology and birdwatching.

The verdict at the inquest was 'accidental death', but the jury added the following rider:

> That we beg to tender our deepest sympathy with the parents of the deceased and also with Mr Kemp and the other members of the staff of the Wireless Telegraph Co. with whom the deceased worked so cordially and we desire to place on record our sorrow at such a tragic ending to so promising a career, connected as it was with one of the most important discoveries of the century'.[5]

The scene now moves to 1973 when Ballycastle Urban District Council decided unanimously to dedicate a plaque commemorating the historic transmissions on the 75th anniversary. Initially, the names of Marconi, Kemp and Glanville were approved by the Council for inclusion on the plaque. There appeared to be some doubt concerning Glanville's actual role in the historic development as a result of which the Council Clerk wrote to the Marconi Company for verification and were informed (as I understand it) that Glanville was doing some other work on Rathlin at the time and was not involved in a wireless test on 21 August – the day of his death.[6] Accordingly, the Council agreed that Marconi and Kemp should be named on the memorial but that Glanville should be named at the ceremony. No blame should be attributed to the Council for this. They were simply acting on the wrong information about Glanville's employment with Marconi. Certainly, the fact that he had been working for the company for well over a year, having started before Kemp, was not mentioned at all to the Council.

The facts are that Marconi himself in the course of his invited paper to the Institution of Electrical Engineers in London, his first in the English language in 1899 explicitly states: 'My assistants Mr Kemp and the late Mr Glanville installed the instruments at Ballycastle and at Rathlin Island.' And further on in the same paragraph:

> At Rathlin we found that the lighthouse keepers were not long in learning how to work the instruments and after the sad accident which happened to poor Mr Glanville, that installation was worked by them alone, there being no expert on the island at the time.[7]

5 H.A. Boyd, 'Marconi and Ballycastle', August 1968.   6 P. Clarke, 'Marconi in Ballycastle / Rathlin Island'.   7 G. Marconi, 'Wireless telegraphy' *Journal of the Institution of Electrical Engineers*, vol. 28 (1899), pp. 273–328.

It would appear that the Marconi Company correspondent had no knowledge of these written statements coming from a prestigious and primary source, Marconi himself. Moreover, 21 August 1898 was a Sunday and Glanville was presumably, with permission, taking a few hours off duty to pursue his interest in geology. Certainly, he was not engaged in other work on that day.[8]

The final episode in this sad saga was the funeral of Edwin Glanville in Dublin as reported in the *Irish Times*, 26 August 1898. A very large number of people attended the final rites at Mount Jerome Cemetery and, as well as the grief-stricken family, Guglielmo Marconi, Jameson Davis and two members of the Goodbody family also attended representing the Marconi Company. Wreaths and floral tributes were also sent by these gentlemen. There was no doubt about the high esteem with which Edwin Glanville had been held by Guglielmo Marconi himself and his close colleagues.

8 In my opinion, it would be fitting even at this late stage (and it should be pointed out that the controversy has been occasionally simmering throughout the years) after the event, if Glanville's proper role could be commemorated, perhaps with a plaque on Rathlin Island itself. The sad fact that he did not live to see the almost unbelievable future of radio communications throughout the twentieth century, in particular the incredible successes of Guglielmo Marconi, makes his contribution of 1898 both at Rathlin and Kingstown very significant indeed. His previous work in England was also noteworthy. This plaque should also include the names of the lighthouse keepers and the Lloyds agent. The Rathlin islanders remember Edwin Glanville to this day and a special commemoration was held on the centenary of his death in August 1998 to which relatives were invited.

CHAPTER 7

Marconi's wireless station, Crookhaven, Co. Cork, 1901–22

Following his spectacular success in England and Ireland, Marconi was acutely conscious of the inescapable truth that the Wireless Telegraph Co. was in a parlous financial state and urgently needed substantial expansion commercially. He had always considered that a successful link with North America was highly desirable, in fact it was his ultimate objective at this time. There were, of course, telegraph cables but these were becoming increasingly overloaded, with inevitable delays and the cost of additional transatlantic cables was simply prohibitive, coupled with the uncertainty of cable breakdown.

Accurate anticipation of the arrival of the transatlantic ships was also a major factor for various commercial reasons and Marconi had already established the feasibility of this with the success of the Ballycastle-Rathlin wireless link. The particular choice of Crookhaven was not simply on account of its location in the extreme south-west tip of Ireland (closest to North America) together with the adjoining Fastnet lighthouse and Cape Clear Island. In fact, since the 1860s these locations had been extensively used by the two well-known companies Reuters and Lloyds for transatlantic ship contact by means of semaphores and even waterproof containers picked up by locally-based small vessels. Furthermore, a telegraph line actually connected Crookhaven with Cork City eighty miles away. It will be shown in Appendix 4 that Marconi was able to dedicate this telegraph line to the wireless station by means of tuned circuits. Crookhaven was, literally, a focus of incoming information from North America by ships and Marconi was very well aware of this existing infrastructure and its potential for further development using wireless. There was nothing haphazard in his choice of this particularly remote and relatively inaccessible place for his first major long-term commercial venture in Ireland following his wireless success with the smaller system between Ballycastle and Rathlin Island. In 1901 the British Post Office under the authority of Preece was controlling communication with Rathlin Island using his short-lived induction method of transmission without wires.

Figure 7.1 Julius Reuter, 1861

Julius Reuter and Crookhaven

Paul Julius Reuter was born in Kassel, Germany in 1816 of Jewish parentage and even in his school years was fascinated by the experiments of Karl Gauss (of Gauss's law fame) who was then experimenting with sending electrical signals by wire. This would have been contemporaneous with Ampère and Faraday.[1]

Reuter's first business adventure was – unbelievably – in the pigeon carrier business when he discovered to his astonishment that there was a 50km 'no go' corridor completely separating the national telegraphic networks of France and Germany. In fact it appeared to be a political open circuit. Reuter was permitted to close this gap between Aachen and Variers in France with pigeons until the wire connections were finally made.

As with Marconi at a later stage, Reuter proceeded to London but was repeatedly rebuffed when he sought employment with *The Times* ('We are not

---

1 Donald Read, *The Power of News: the History of Reuters, 1849–1989* (Oxford: Oxford University Press, 1992); Alfred O'Mahony, 'Julius Reuter in Ireland', *Journal of the Mizen Archaeological and Historical Society* 8/28 (2000). Karl Friedrich Gauss (1777–1855) passed all his working life at Gottingen University, specialising in astronomy, physics and with a very strong interest in pure *and* applied mathematics. In the latter context his work on the relations between electric charges and forces was a milestone in electromagnetism. In stature Gauss bears comparison with Newton and is recognised as such in the scientific world: T.E. Williams (ed.), *A Biographical Dictionary of Scientists* (London: Adam and Charles Black, 1969).

Figure 7.2 Meeting the mail boat at Cape Race, Newfoundland, 1861. This was very similar to the operation involving Crookhaven, Cape Clear and Fastnet – and just as dangerous.

prepared to enter into any arrangement with you', was the haughty response). Not to be outdone Reuter opened offices in Marseilles, Lisbon and Trieste where his agents processed news from the Middle East, South America and the Far East respectively. This earned him world-wide contracts from Lloyds and as would be expected, *The Times* had to swallow its pride for its previous rejection of Reuter's requests for work. Reuter was already following a long-term strategy whereby he hoped to acquire contracts from the British Government to link all the major colonies of the British Empire telegraphically to London and in this he was ultimately successful. Subsequently, in the 1920s, Marconi also had considerable success in modernising this empire network using short wave radio which he had developed experimentally using his yacht *Elettra* as a floating laboratory.

Reuter opened a telegraphic agency in London in 1851 and extended his agency to Derry and Queenstown (now Cobh) in 1853. Next followed an independent company known as the 'Telegraph Dispatch' based in Cork which regularly sent a tender with reporters from many agencies on board to meet incoming liners or freight ships from North America at the mouth of Cork Harbour. A major drawback usually arose when the reporters returned to Cork by train (about 12 miles upstream) resulting in an unholy, if not unseemly, scramble to monopolise the telegraph line to London. After surveying this chaotic scene for some time Julius Reuter hit upon an utterly simple but totally effective means of overcoming the 'army' of his competitors, viz: if he could meet the ships off Cape Clear/Fastnet lighthouse some eighty miles from Cork, he would have a four-hour lead in telegraphing his transatlantic information to London (usually Fleet Street) from Crookhaven itself. This entrepreneuring spirit displayed by Reuter was worthy of Marconi himself over thirty years later.

Accordingly, Reuter formally obtained approval to form the 'Southwest of Ireland Telegraph Company' and immediately commenced building the eighty-mile telegraph line from Crookhaven to Cork. Serious objections came from the *Cork Examiner* in July 1863 which denounced Reuter as a 'clever foreign specu-lator' who was determined to monopolise the foreign news. However, two days later the *Skibbereen Eagle* (that sturdy paper which subsequently chastised no less a personage than the Czar of Russia for the alleged political murder of the Emperor of China which turned out to be false with the warning to 'keep its eye on him'), praised the 'Telegraph King' who after all, was offering employment to the inhabitants of the remote Mizen Peninsula area.[2]

The Crookhaven-Cork telegraph began operating in December 1863 and Reuter closed the telegraphic 'loop' by leasing a compact steamer, the *Marseilles*, which plied between Crookhaven and the transatlantic steamers. One of the most dramatic telegrams received from the SS *Australasia* off Crookhaven summarised the fall of the Confederate capital Richmond, Virginia at the end of the American Civil War in April 1865 (see page 20 above). Note that the total time for the telegraph to be processed and received in London from New York was 9 days (5–14 April). As well as describing the carnage of the siege, the price standard of gold is given as $148\frac{5}{8}$. A second telegram brought by the SS *Asia* to Crookhaven announced the surrender of General Robert E. Lee on 13 April 1865, the gold standard now being $146\frac{1}{8}$. Presumably it dropped when the war ended.

The importance of the Crookhaven station at this particular time was consid-erably enhanced by trade news from America especially relating to the cotton crop in Georgia and the tobacco plantations in Virginia both of which were devastated during the war, leading in particular to large-scale unemployment in the cotton mills of Lancashire. In fact, the stock exchange began to depend on Reuters to inform it of the latest fluctuations in war or in trade in the United States.

Reuters worked in tandem with Lloyds of London who informed them of the expected arrival in Irish waters of ships travelling in both directions. Foggy weather was a real problem and the best that could be done was for Lloyds employees on Cape Clear to listen for ships' horn blasts and then sally forth to locate the ships. Phosphorescent lights on the news containers thrown overboard were some help but the whole technique – if one can call it that – was obviously a hit-and-miss affair and, of course, occasionally dangerous especially in stormy weather.

2 L. O'Regan, *Eye on Russia: Its History* Southern Star Centenary, 1899–1999, p. 56.

Figure 7.3 Crookhaven in 1900/1 facing west towards the Atlantic Ocean. Marconi's original aerial mast (arrowed) was located behind the present Marconi House, where he stayed at the entrance to the village. The Brow Head installation was subsequently built for far better reception. The headland itself is faintly visible in the background.

Reuter originally had a telegraphic station on Cape Clear for direct transmission of the messages retrieved from the sea. However, an underwater cable to the mainland was obviously desirable, but rock and rough seas effectively marooned Cape Clear in inclement weather (for example, during the disastrous storm during the Cowes–Fastnet yacht race in 1979 when fifteen yachtsmen were drowned in mountainous seas). Eventually Cape Clear was reduced to a secondary station and Crookhaven itself was chosen, as already mentioned, together with the compact steamer *Marseilles* to meet the incoming ships.

After several abortive attempts the Atlantic was finally traversed successfully by cable in 1866 but, due to a phenomenal increase in telegram traffic arising from the massive increase in cable networks, activities at Crookhaven continued to flourish. Another factor favouring Crookhaven was that the anticipated arrival time of the ships in the UK could be determined within a matter of hours, whereas notification via cable from North America only could be up to several days in uncertainty of the Atlantic weather. Indeed, sea traffic near the Fastnet was so great towards the end of the nineteenth century that Lloyds bought additional land in 1882 at the summit of Brow Head, 300 feet above sea level, approximately two miles west of Crookhaven. This is where Marconi located his wireless station over twenty years later. In 1884, an undersea cable seven miles long reconnected the Fastnet with the mainland and this now included an Edison telephone system for the first time. As with previous underwater cables there were the usual unpredictable breakages, but, with improved insulation, the venture was successful enough to warrant the attention of the British Post Office under the Telegraph Act of 1868. However, a new player in the shape of the British Admiralty, which had a large base only thirty sea miles from the Fastnet at Berehaven, Bantry Bay, objected to the PO monopoly and the matter was actually discussed in the parliament in London. Faced with further opposition from the Lighthouse Institution (Trinity House, London) the Post Office backed off, but as we have seen, reactivated its claim during Marconi's wireless operations over twenty years later at Ballycastle.

Reuters has been on the world scene now for 150 years and a glance at any current newspaper will demonstrate its continuing news-gathering activities. The story which began with carrier pigeons connecting the cable telegraphy systems of two countries has now reached the age of communication satellites taking full advantage of the revolution in communication technology. Even towards the end of the nineteenth century it had attained international recognition for bridging the Atlantic to establish reliable contacts with the New World and there is little doubt but that the major telegraph terminus for transatlantic communications via ships at Crookhaven together with its ancillary outposts on the Fastnet lighthouse, Cape Clear and Brow Head was a significant factor in ultimately achieving global recognition. In addition Reuters' formal association with another major international marine player (Lloyds) was also noteworthy and in the case of Crookhaven the involvement of Trinity House London which controlled the Fastnet Lighthouse and all the lighthouses around the coasts of the British Isles was an additional positive factor.

The advent of Marconi's wireless station at Crookhaven, Co. Cork
In 1901 Guglielmo Marconi opened another chapter in the history of Crookhaven's involvement in communication by setting up a wireless transmit/receive station to replace the existing somewhat unreliable inshore cable systems where possible, and establish two-way wireless from ship-to-shore using Brow Head as the station site and the Fastnet lighthouse, also equipped with wireless, as the first contact with the incoming transatlantic ships.[3] He already had considerable experience arising from his activities at Ballycastle, Kingstown and several locations in England, notably, the Isle of Wight and adjacent lighthouses. By 1899 Marconi had set up twenty such wireless stations on the southern English

---

3 M.C. Sexton, 'Marconi's wireless telegraphy station at Crookhaven', *Journal of the Mizen Archaeological and Historical Society*, 3/79 (1995).

coastline and this was followed by installations not only at Crookhaven but also at Malin Head, Co. Donegal, and Rosslare, Co. Wexford, which had telegraph connections nearby. These latter stations were technically similar to the Crookhaven facility and used for commercial shipping only.

At that time Marconi was keenly interested in improving safety at sea, hence his contacts with Trinity House which controlled the lighthouses, and with the marine specialists Lloyds of London. Moreover it was virtually certain that wireless installation would become mandatory on ships permitting direct contacts with land receivers e.g. Crookhaven. The ill-fated *Titanic* in 1912 was a major boost for the fortunes of the Marconi Wireless Telegraph Company, leading to its share – previously unsaleable at 50p – rocketing almost overnight to £10 [today, €500].

Irish stations were quite similar in design, and attention will be concentrated on Crookhaven which up to the advent of Clifden, Co. Galway, in 1907 was the most noteworthy. However, it is worth recording that the news of President Lincoln's assassination in April 1865 was first reported via canisters to Reuters telegraph office in Derry from Malin Head.

The transmitting/receiving equipment on Brow Head was in accordance with the technology of the time, noting that the coherer in the receiver was replaced by the much faster magnetic detector in 1902 (see Appendix 4).

The Crookhaven station got off to a flying start in June 1901 when, soon after its opening and in the presence of Marconi himself, Morse signals were received

Figure 7.4 The wireless transmitter and receiver systems on Brow Head, Crookhaven

strongly and clearly from Poldhu in Cornwall, 225 miles distant. This not only confirmed the station's range as being the planned 300 miles, using a spark gap transmitter and coherer detector, but the received signals were of such strength that Marconi felt quite confident of 'bridging the Atlantic' – which he duly did only six months later. Of far more significance, however, was the fact that the signals were actually received at all, since it was generally accepted at that time that, following the theory of Maxwell and the experiments of Hertz, electromagnetic radiation proceeded in straight lines. In the Poldhu–Crookhaven test the rays had clearly followed the curvature of the earth. This indisputable fact convinced Marconi of the likely feasibility of his transatlantic link. We now know that the earth is, in fact, encircled by several ionospheric layers of ionised particles ranging from 50 to 300km high which reflect the straight line rays back to the earth. The occasional signal fading of conventional short wave radio reception, which depends entirely on ionospheric reflection to cover the long distances, is due to vertical movement of the layers over a 24-hour period.[4]

It is clear that Marconi spent at least three periods of several weeks in Crookhaven, surviving two train journeys of broad and narrow gauge/jaunting car/ferry twice on each occasion from Cork – a total round journey of 160 miles. He also called at the offices of the *Cork Examiner*, mindful of the hostile reception which the paper had given to Reuter in 1863. On this occasion he was warmly welcomed.

It is difficult to obtain authoritative information on what exactly was accomplished by the Marconi personnel at Crookhaven, especially since the whole region incorporating Crookhaven/Brow Head on land and Cape Clear/Fastnet offshore had previously been utilised by Reuters, Lloyds, the Royal Navy and the British Post Office trying to assert its monopoly. To make matters still more complicated (or as the mathematicians say: non-linear) a Napoleonic signal watch tower dating from 1807 is still on Brow Head. This was to give early warning of an anticipated second French invasion. The previous attempt in 1796 was a serious affair and only bad weather prevented no less than 20,000 troops from disembarking in Bantry Bay.

Notwithstanding the scarcity of information, the Marconi Company in Chelmsford holds a paper written in 1911 by W.H. Leach, then one of the Morse operators at Crookhaven. The following extracts give a perceptive insight into the working of the station at that time as well as the general ambience of Crookhaven itself.[5]

4 A. Guagnini and G. Pancaldi, *Cento di Anni di Radio: Le radici dell'invenzione* (Torino, SEAT, 1995).
5 H.W. Leach, 'In Human Element at the Wireless Station: Life at Crookhaven', *The Marconigraph*, p. 23, September 1911.

Figure 7.5 Brow Head station during World War I. The caption reads 'War Signal Station, Brow Head', with sailors from the Royal Navy in the foreground.

There were at that date [wrote Leach] few sea-going vessels fitted with wireless apparatus, and the comparatively easy life of the operator on duty there in those days may be gauged from the fact that fifty messages from in-going and out-going steamers was considered a great feat. The actual telegraphic work was hardly sufficient to keep the operators busy at all times, but in following the developments in wireless telegraphy these operators were kept constantly interested. A change has, however, come over the place. The magnetic detector has been introduced, and Crookhaven has sprung into prominence as a wireless station. By reason of its geographical situation, all ships coming from the west and bound for a European port enter into communication with Crookhaven, and that station is busily employed, night and day, in sending and receiving messages. The life lived by the operators at this station is now a strenuous, albeit an interesting one. One incident, although it occurred nearly seven years ago, may be recalled as serving to show what was in the early days regarded as a welcome relief from the monotony of life in a station not busily employed. In 1904 an Atlantic liner, equipped with Marconi apparatus, broke one of her shafts some eighty miles out. Communication was at once set up between the station and the disabled liner, and over one hundred messages were cleared, the majority being to friends of the passengers in different parts of the world, and others summoning assistance, which was speedily rendered. For twenty-four hours the operators were busily engaged, and with the aid of wireless telegraphy the liner was ultimately enabled to continue upon her voyage. But times have changed; Crookhaven Station no longer waits for a chance event to stimulate activity, for the regular passage to and from steamers keeps the station incessantly engaged in receiving commercial and personal messages from those on board.

The life of an operator at Crookhaven differs greatly from the life of an operator at sea. There is little variety or excitement in the life, but the experienced gained is both novel and interesting. The first impression on arriving at the village of Crookhaven is that the 'end of everywhere' has been reached. But all sense of solitude vanishes before the pleasant and cheerful welcome received from one's colleagues, and the newcomer finds himself – for some time, at any rate – the centre of local interest.

There are usually six operators at this station. The day is divided into three watches, viz., midnight to 8 a.m. to 4 p.m. to midnight, two operators being required on each watch. The daily routine proceeds with but little change. Every evening at about eleven o'clock the operators on the midnight to 8 a.m. prepare for their tramp to the station stands on Brow Head, the most south-westerly point of Ireland, at an altitude over 300ft. The road from the village runs some distance along the shore, then rises

Figure 7.6 Picture taken by Mr P. Clarke of RTÉ *c.*1980 clearly showing the aerial mast foundation in the foreground and the still-standing ruin of the power generating housing. All that now remains of the latter is an unrecognisable mound of rubble (2004).

abruptly along the edge of the cliffs to the top of Brow Head. The absence of any signs of life on this road accentuates the encircling gloom. Rarely, if ever, is the solitude of the traveller broken by the chance meeting of a fellow creature; no light save that figuratively derived from the stars softens the blackness of the night, which is intermittently penetrated by the rays from the Fastnet Lighthouse, situated about seven miles off the mainland. At the station, however, the operator feels that he is again swept into the busy world. He will probably find that a dozen or more ships are in communication with the station, and will be kept busy sending and receiving messages form these ships. As Crookhaven is the first station with which the homeward-bound American liners communicate it is naturally a busy station. By the aid of wireless all arrangements are made for the arrival of the ships, the landing and entraining of the passengers and mails, whilst hundreds of private messages to and from passengers are dealt with. Messages are also received from the Fastnet Lighthouse, which is fitted with wireless, reporting the passing of sailing ships and steamers. These messages are sent by vessels not fitted with wireless by means of signals to the Fastnet, thence by wireless to Crookhaven, whence they are forwarded to Lloyd's [*sic*] and to the owners of the vessels.

The tremendous advance made in wireless during the past few years is strikingly illustrated by a comparison of the present-day working at Crookhaven with that of earlier days. Some six or seven years ago it was quite unusual to be in communication with more than one ship at a time, and occasionally periods of one and even two days passed without any communications being handled. Today, Crookhaven is always in communication with at least six ships, and sometimes with as many as twenty. The operating is now carried on at over twice the speed using magnetic detectors and the distance of communication is greatly increased. Under these conditions the operator is kept busily engaged throughout his watch.

No discussion on Marconi's Crookhaven station would be complete without reference to Arthur (Daddy) Nottage, the Englishman who became both a legend and an institution in his own lifetime in Crookhaven – indeed in West Cork – where he lived amongst friends for some seventy years, being the owner of the Welcome Inn public house. He had an extraordinary career and indeed as a youth of only twenty was a major link between Europe and North America via incoming ships passing Crookhaven. He found himself in the exalted position in 1904 when he arrived in Crookhaven to work, on a shift basis with one other man, as a Marconi telegrapher. Until 1914 he operated the Morse code apparatus from Brow Head, with his salary for such responsible work being a reputed generous £1 per week.[6]

The photograph (figure 7.7) shows Nottage in the doorway of the Welcome Inn in 1961 with the premises temporarily renamed for the making of a film entitled *I Thank a Fool* with Susan Hayward and Peter Finch in the leading roles. The presence of 100 people working on the film for several weeks in Crookhaven certainly enlivened the village.

By 1914 the Crookhaven station was beginning to lose its usefulness, mainly on account of its limited range, and it is understood that Marconi sold the wireless rights to Cable & Wireless Ltd on Valentia Island, Co. Kerry. In that year, however, the First World War gave it a new lease of life when the British Post Office finally succeeded in acquiring the station and leased it to the Royal Navy. However, the Royal Navy had been using its facilities occasionally since the commissioning of the station in 1901. This connection with the large navy base in Berehaven, Bantry Bay, approximately thirty sea miles from Crookhaven, had disastrous consequences for Crookhaven. The station was destroyed in 1922 by Republican forces opposing the Anglo-Irish Treaty of 1921. Its known involvement with the Royal Navy, which retained the base at Berehaven by the

6 I met Mr Nottage in Crookhaven some years before his death at the age of 90 in 1974. He still had hand-written log books from the station recording the daily events and explained the workings of wireless during that far-off period to a very interested audience that day in the Welcome Inn.

Figure 7.7 Arthur Nottage, one of the more celebrated Morse operators at the Crookhaven station in the early 20th century, seen here at the door of his 'Welcome Inn' renamed temporarily in 1961 for a film.

terms of the same treaty until 1938, was almost certainly a major factor in the destruction. All that remains intact at present is the antenna foundation on which the youngest daughter of Marconi, Princess Elettra unveiled a commemorative plaque in 1998. Thus ended the short lived (1901–22) but intriguing existence of Crookhaven wireless station. It was a major element in Julius Reuter's telegraphic contact with North America via ships, beginning in 1863, and the subsequent location of Marconi's station, these taking advantage of the then existing infrastructure which clearly shows Marconi's extremely sharp commercial enterprise, especially relating to his successful pre-transatlantic tests between Poldhu and Crookhaven in June 1901 which subsequently culminated in the massive undertaking at Clifden, Co. Galway, in 1907.

CHAPTER 8

The great leap (*il grande salto*) across the Atlantic from Ireland to Canada

Marconi's great dream was to transmit and receive wireless signals across the Atlantic and the test at Crookhaven was a major boost to his confidence – if this was indeed necessary. Apart from the real engineering risks involved, this would be a major financial undertaking on both sides of the Atlantic and he had considerable difficulty in persuading the board of directors to allocate scarce company resources to this nebulous project, especially when they believed that there would be a steady if unspectacular guaranteed income from his less ostentatious marine activities. Marconi's cousin Jameson Davis, the only other engineer director, used all his influence to win over his staid grain merchant colleagues. However, the young man who had, only six years previously in 1895, overcome similar opposition from his father eventually obtained grudging backing from his fellow directors. But, although Marconi had successfully commissioned small stations such as Ballycastle and Crookhaven with a certain amount of 'home-made' equipment, the obstacles that the signals would now have to surmount were not a few hills and expanses of water but the mind-boggling 'mountain' of the Atlantic Ocean, bulging nearly 150 miles high between England and North America.

Since the Maxwell theory of the 1860s that electromagnetic waves, of which light was the only known one at that time, all travelled in straight lines, the only significant variable being the wavelength, they could not penetrate much beyond the optical horizon. But Marconi now had, in his own opinion and with supreme confidence, enough evidence by 1900 from ship-to-ship and ship-to-shore communication *over the horizon* as well as the Poldhu–Crookhaven test in June 1901, to indicate that there was more to the process than the simple optical transmission analogy. In turn this led him inevitably to the probable future of long-distance wireless communications in direct competition with the cable companies and, again with supreme confidence (some would say arrogance), he considered the problem to be solely a matter of increasing the power transmitted and developing more sensitive receivers.

These requirements lifted the engineering effort to a much higher plane,

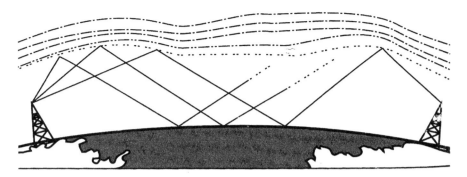

Figure 8.1 The transatlantic experiment: two continents joined by an electromagnetic wave

Table C *Experimental Stations specifically adapted for the First Transatlantic Transmission*

Lizard, Cornwall	January 1901
Poldhu, Cornwall	January 1901
Crookhaven, Co. Cork, Ireland	June 1901
Cape Cod, Massachusetts, USA.	June 1901
Signal Hill, Newfoundland, Canada	
(substituting Cape Cod)	September 1901

requiring a virtual industrial complex to generate the tens of transmission kilowatts of electrical power and truly enormous antennae at Clifden. This, in turn, needed additional professional staff of high calibre. Foremost amongst this élite was Professor Alexander Fleming of London University, who had considerable expertise not only in antenna design but also in the powerful transmitters needed. It was intended that extremely weak signals should be received from transmitters thousands of miles distant.[1]

The Poldhu site at the extremity of Cornwall had been acquired in October 1900, together with the North American site at Cape Cod, Massachusetts, with nothing but water between them. Construction of the stations began simultaneously on both sides but disaster struck at Poldhu in the form of a gale which flattened the huge circular antenna with its gasometer-like structure. Worse was to follow in November 1900 when another gale destroyed the Cape Cod antenna. Marconi's great scheme to transmit between the two stations of the old and new worlds had collapsed.

---

1 P.K. Bondyopadhyay, 'Fleming and Marconi: the co-operation of the century', *Radio Scientist* (URSI) 5/2, June 1994.

Figure 8.2 The antenna system of the Transatlantic station at Poldhn, Cornwall, 1902

Figure 8.3 Marconi and his assistants putting up a kite at Signal Hill, Newfoundland to receive signals from Poldhn in December 1901

Marconi faced a storm of criticism from his directors on account of the huge financial loss but, with dogged determination, succeeded in assembling a smaller antenna at Poldhu and moving as near as possible to Cornwall by relocating at Signal Hill, St John's, Newfoundland. All that could be put together was a receiving contraption of balloons and kites to raise the aerial wire as high as possible. The transatlantic test was, in effect, back to the Villa Griffone style of experiments of 1895, notwithstanding the secret commercial planning and the unmentionable expense.

Finally, on 12 December 1901, all seemed to be in order at Signal Hill and Marconi sent a cablegram to Poldhu arranging that signals be transmitted at specified times consisting of the three dots representing the letter S in the Morse Code. But their old enemy – the weather – struck again and deteriorated to such an extent that a balloon and kite had to be replaced (no mean feat in the Canadian winter) with Marconi's assistant Kemp having to struggle to hang on to the balloon's guide line. Notwithstanding these adverse conditions Marconi managed to detect the S-dots on 12 December over the crackling atmospherics, followed by somewhat weaker signals on the following day. These signals would never have been received with a conventional coherer or magnetic detector but Marconi had been given a more sensitive detector using a special mercury contact designed by his old colleague Luigi Solari of the Italian Navy.

Notwithstanding the almost universal acclaim which greeted the extraordinary feat, some reservations were immediately expressed as to whether what was received was merely noise from the atmospheric background – from thunderstorms occurring over the 2,500-mile 'jump'. This was compounded by the fact that there was no printed record of the reception and only two witnesses – Marconi and Kemp – who could hardly be considered impartial by the cynics. I retain a lingering doubt also, but it must be stated that the reproduction of the *same* signal on consecutive days at the *specified* times makes it highly improbable that the signals originated from the *random* electrical and naturally occurring noise. (This point is illustrated by tuning in to the medium or shortwave bands in a conventional radio during a thunderstorm.) However, even if the signals had been of atmospheric origin, there is absolutely no doubt about the signals received during Marconi's return voyage to England on the SS *Philadelphia* in January 1902, when they were unambiguously recorded both by day and night as soon as the ship had left New York – several thousand miles from Poldhu. Marconi had shown convincingly that long distance over-the-horizon wireless communication was possible and a completely new era of information transfer was opened up.

One fascinating question relating to the historic experiments was to determine exactly what was happening to reflect the wireless waves back to earth. The key lay in the differing levels of reception by day and night. This indicated clearly that the sun was playing a significant role and in 1902, Heaviside and Kennelly independently suggested that the sun was ionising the atmosphere (detaching electrons from the neutral atoms/molecules of nitrogen, oxygen etcetera in the upper atmosphere) into various concentrated layers 50–300km from the earth and that the free electrons in the layers were the cause of the reflections. The actual layers were the results of the earth's *gravitational* field attracting the heavy molecular ions (N2+, O2+ etc) near to the earth whereas the lighter atomic ions (N+, O+ etc) tended to concentrate at higher levels where the atmospheric pressure was considerably lower than that on earth.[2]

Kennelly and Heaviside, and later Appleton, were quite correct in their suggestion and this initiated the new branch of ionospheric physics which is still a very fruitful field of research today. The use of rockets after the Second World War enabled scientists to examine the structure of the layers for the first time, and laboratory simulation of the ionospheric gas interaction with radio waves was another key development. It is well known that long distance shortwave radio propagation is due entirely to ionospheric reflection and the physical movement of the layers is the cause of temporary radio fading of the transmissions. In the 1920s Marconi, as would be expected, made full use of the ionosphere for successful world-wide transmissions.

The transition from the 'hit or miss' test between Poldhu and Signal Hill in 1901 to a fully operational commercial undertaking, which had already cost far more than originally envisaged, was to prove even more costly and, worse still, a lengthy affair since Marconi had to increase and stabilise transmitter power and design suitable *directional* antennae. It was essential to focus the wireless beam ideally like an optical searchlight in order to have a reasonable hope of meaningful reception in North America. However, at this stage (*c.*1902) a fundamental mistake was made by concentrating on even longer wavelengths than hitherto employed as the 'trial and error' tests appeared to indicate that this was the way forward for long-distance communications. In turn this implied tuned antenna systems of the order of kilometres in length. For example, the 50khz frequency corresponds to a wavelength of 6km. This immediately eliminated Poldhu on the basis of the need for several square kilometres of antenna area. (A current example of large antenna areas would be the LW BBC Radio 4, operating at 198khz corresponding to a wavelength of 1.5km.)

Notwithstanding this, Marconi continued to put considerable effort into

2 Although Kennelly and Heaviside are usually credited with the proposal for reflecting ionised layers in the upper atmosphere it had actually been suggested in 1878 by Balfour Stewart that small daily variations in the earth's magnetic field implied that sheets of electrically charged particles circulate horizontally high above the earth (the dynamo theory). This appeared in the *Encyclopedia Britannica* (9th edition, vol. 16, 1883.) It should also be noted that one of the later ionospheric scientists was Joseph Larmor of Queen's University, Belfast.

Figure 8.4 Marconi in the operations room at Glace Bay

developing the transatlantic link, spurred on by the knowledge that spanning the Atlantic without the problems of an undersea cable was very attractive indeed, bearing in mind the ever-increasing flow of information, both commercial and private and, of course, the almost certain lucrative rewards for the Marconi Company.

However, the actual commercialisation of the wireless link to a trustworthy level proved to be even more complicated than envisaged. In fact *the* major problem that now emerged was that the experimenters simply did not know the frequencies being generated which, of course, had insurmountable consequences for tuned fixed dimension antennae with their enormous size, as well as for tuned receivers. Again, Sir Alexander Fleming was of assistance in developing frequency meters, later followed by another Marconi consultant, Thomas Round, who subsequently extended the frequency metre design to high frequencies when it was realised eventually that this was the only way to extend the range of operation. (Thomas Round is well known for his development of the FM discriminator in modern VHF receivers in 1935.) Until Fleming's perfection of the frequency metre, trial and error was the order of the day – usually more error than trial.

Marconi's transatlantic wireless station, Clifden, Co. Galway
By 1905 Marconi felt confident enough to search for a suitable site with sufficient ground area to replace Poldhu. He chose the west coast of Ireland, since it was as near as possible to Canada, and in July of that year finally settled on 120 hectares of bogland at Derrygimla, three miles south of Clifden, Co. Galway, which itself is some fifty miles west of Galway City. Clifden was linked to Galway

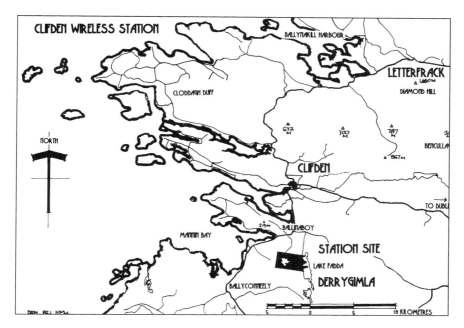

Figure 8.5 Location of the Clifden wireless station at Derrygimla, Co. Galway

by both rail and telegraphic connections. Apart from having a direct view of the Atlantic Ocean, the site also had about twenty years of good quality turf from the bog which could be used as fuel, together with a lake for supplying and cooling the steam boilers for driving the electrical generators. In addition, the site was only approximately eighty miles from Dromoland Castle in Co. Clare, which was the ancestral home of Beatrice O'Brien, daughter of Baron Inchiquin and Marconi's first wife, whom he married in 1905. This connection would have made the presence of this 'semi-Italian foreigner', whose mother after all was Irish, more acceptable than might otherwise have been the case in this very remote area. It might also be added that a small, but finite, element of altruism may have crept into Marconi's thoughts about the location.

The remoteness of Derrygimla was clearly and succinctly summarised by Marconi's eldest daughter Degna, born in 1908, in the biography of her father published in 1962: 'Clifden was only the address as the wireless station was miles from any town and so isolated on the spongy bogs that it could only be reached by trollies on rails. Cold dampness rose from the marshes and saturated everything, making even lighting a fire a problem'.[3] On the other hand Marconi's second wife, Maria Cristina Bezzi-Scala, whom he married in 1927 (having

3 Degna Marconi, *My Father Marconi*.

Figure 8.6 The Marconi wireless station, Clifden, Connemara, 1908. The large building in the centre housed the condenser system for tuning the transmitter.

divorced Beatrice in 1924), writing, in 1995, her memories of her husband remarked about Clifden: '*Era situato in una pianura sull' incantevole costa irlanda* [It was situated in a plain on the wonderful (or enchanting) coast of Ireland]'.[4]

The building of the station at Clifden commenced in October 1905 and, right from the beginning, the sheer magnitude of the undertaking became obvious on account of the 45khz transmitting frequency corresponding to a wavelength of 6.7km. Whereas a radio station at present requires a substantial land area, the magnitude of the Clifden station is difficult to visualise, with the site occupying almost 2.5 square kms and a directional transmitting antenna system almost 1km long consisting initially of 8 wooden (later steel) masts, each 64m high, linked by wires attached to large concrete blocks. An earthing system was provided by a copper mesh 180m long and 1.2m wide, buried under the line of the antenna wires. Furthermore, this mesh had to be positioned across a small lake in the line of the antennae. The receiving antenna consisted of four wires in parallel, supported at the tops of the transmitting antenna.

The steam-driven generator plant produced an output of 300kw of electric power to send the spark-generated wireless signal across the Atlantic using no less than 20kv in a rotary spark gap generator actually developed by Marconi himself. In terms of efficiency and audibility of the signal, this was a major improvement over the single spark used in ships but, more importantly, it could handle the enormous power that seemed to be necessary to span the Atlantic at low frequencies. However, the great advantage of the rotary spark generator was

4 Maria Christina Marconi, *Mio Marito, Guglielmo* (Milan: Rizzoli, 1995).

Figure 8.7 Electrical machinery in the power house at Clifden

that it effectively produced continuous oscillations, since the oscillating time decay of the sparks overlapped, permitting fine tuning at the receiving end – hence the name 'singing spark'. In fact, Marconi's development of the rotary spark generator proved to be the zenith of spark transmission.[5] By 1918, thermionic valves such as the diode, developed by Sir Alexander Fleming, and the triode, developed by Lee de Forest (along with numerous patent legal wrangles), were replacing the essential elements in the transmitters and receivers, leading ultimately to shortwave transmission in the 1920s.

In order to tune the inductive circuit transmitter to 45kz with a capacitive element, a gigantic condenser with 1800 plates of galvanised iron and using air dielectric between the plates, produced the required capacitance of 1.8 micro-farads. This had to be housed in a separate building 107m x 23m x 10m. Nowadays using modern dielectric materials between the plates, the overall size of the capacitor system would be measured in single figures at most. It must also be remembered that Marconi's condenser system had to withstand 20kv between the plates.

As if this was not enough, a light railway system (2ft gauge) was laid down to

5 P.R. Jensen, *In Marconi's Footsteps, 1894-1920* (Kenthouse, NSW: Kangaroo Press, 1994).

Figure 8.8 The tuning air condenser at Clifden with a capacity of 1.8 microfarads. Note the relative sizes of the workers. Nowadays, with modern dielectric materials, the condenser would have the dimensions of a suitcase.

transport turf from the bog directly to the boilers and to connect with the nearby main road from Clifden to transport supplies, equipment etc.

Work was also proceeding simultaneously on the other side of the Atlantic with a very similar situation at Glace Bay until, at last, in October 1907, a regular and reliable service to Canada and the United States was inaugurated. Congratulatory telegrams were sent by Lloyd George, the President of the UK Board of Trade, to his opposite number in Canada stating that 'all well-wishers of the Empire will welcome every project for facilitating contact between Britain and the Great Dominion across the Atlantic'. Not to be outdone, an outspoken message was subsequently sent by Mr Henry Murphy of Galway County Council to President Theodore Roosevelt, congratulating him on his election as President and seeking assistance to obtain Home Rule for Ireland.[6]

From the commercial aspect the Clifden station was a resounding success from its inception, as Marconi was able to give the faster service of thirty instead of twenty-two words per minute for the cable companies, since the latter were constrained by the immense length of cable and its associated capacitive problems. Far more important, however, was the reduction in charges by a factor of two, with 'Marconigrams' costing 5*d.* per word for ordinary messages and 2½*d.* per word for press reports [today, 78 or 39 cent]. The Marconi Company began to make a profit on the Clifden-Glace Bay link almost immediately, which in all probability saved it from looming bankruptcy.

The world's first point-to-point fixed wireless operation was now successfully installed. In a manner similar to Crookhaven a telegraphic land line laid to Galway was initially used for onward transmission to London, but a permanent line to London was brought into operation in 1908. At the other side of the Atlantic a line was installed to New York from Glace Bay via Montreal since most of the telegraphic traffic, as would be expected, was between London and New York.

Clifden ancillary stations at Letterfrack, Co. Galway, and Ballybunion, Co. Kerry
Initially the Clifden–Glace Bay link worked by means of the 'simplex' system of operation which involved alternate use of the transmitter and receiver so that simultaneous transmission and reception was not possible. With the ever-increasing Marconigram traffic, it was decided in 1911 to convert to 'duplex' operation and a new receiving-only station, connected by land line to Derrygimla, was installed at Letterfrack, ten miles north of Clifden, which also had a clear path for the reception to the Atlantic. Although the structure at Letterfrack was a fairly substantial unit, with eighty men employed in its

---

6 P. Clarke, 'Marconi's Irish Connections Recalled', *100 Years of Radio*, IEE Conference, publication 411, September 1995.

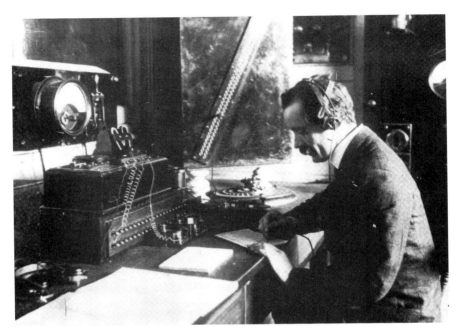

Figure 8.9 Operation at the Marconi station, Clifden, using a magnetic detector (seen on top of the receiver), 1908. For a description of the magnetic detector see Appendix 4.

construction, it was, surprisingly, not economic and was closed down after some years, with the wireless operators returning to Derrygimla. No trace remains today in Letterfrack of this ancillary station.

The second ancillary station associated with Clifden was established in Ballybunion, also in 1912, and directly linked to a similar station in Louisville, Nova Scotia, which was also, of course, under the control of the main station at Glace Bay some forty miles distant. Ballybunion has a historic niche all to itself with the most noteworthy achievement in wireless telephony of transmitting speech to Louisburg in 1919, 1800 miles distant, using thermionic triode valves in the special transmitter and a power supplied of only 2.5kw. Although Reginald Fessenden in the USA had been experimenting successfully with wireless telephony for many years, using ever higher frequency alternators, this Ballybunion transmission would appear to have been Marconi's first serious effort at telephony made possible by the thermionic valves (and sounding the death knell of the spark) and, ultimately leading to shortwave operation in the 1920s in which Marconi played the major world-wide role.[7] For the record, the

7 J.S. Belrose, 'Fessenden and the early history of radio science', *Radio Scientist* (URSI) 5/3, September 1994.

Figure 8.10 General view of the power house and antennae at the Marconi
radio station, Ballybunion, Co. Kerry, March 1919

Figure 8.11 Transmitter installed at Marconi radio station, Ballybunion, March 1919.
Note the inclusion of thermionic valves.

wavelength used at Ballybunion was 3,800m, corresponding to a frequency of 79khz.

The success at Ballybunion led Marconi to go one step further, with a historic first broadcast from his Chelmsford transmitter of the soprano Dame Nellie Melba in 1920. Indeed it might be remarked that this was a forerunner of the British Broadcasting Company (now Corporation) which commenced operations in 1922.

At its peak period of operation the Clifden station employed a permanent staff of 150, together with a temporary staff of approximately 140 – mainly for turf-cutting and turf-drying from March to September. The permanent staff included ten engineers and twenty-five wireless operators working eight-hours shifts over a 24-hour period. Although most of the professional engineering and operator staff came from England, the skilled operatives – fitters, boiler, maintenance men etc. – came from all over Ireland, with labourers coming from the immediate neighbourhood. This considerable employment, together with the supply of goods and services, made a substantial impact on the general standard of living in the Clifden area, ravaged by famine a mere sixty years previously, and had endured soul-destroying emigration as well as the dreadful evictions. The

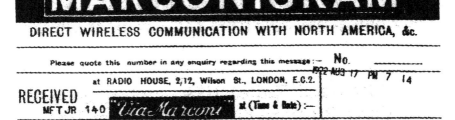

Figure 8.12 The last 'Marconigram' from the Clifden station, 7:14 p.m., 17 August 1922

Figure 8.13 Clifden has another claim to fame, since on 15 June 1919 Captain Alcock and Lieut. Brown crash-landed on a bog at Derrygimla after an epic first transatlantic flight from St Johns, Newfoundland. Their Vickers' Vimy biplane ended up yards from the condenser house, narrowly avoiding a tragic ending.

Clifden area was, in fact, unique in the west of Ireland for its relative affluence at this time.

The station was profitable from the beginning and the Marconi Company was unchallenged in its business with North America. However, the Company set up another station in Caernarvon, Wales in 1914, and from 1918 onwards an increasing amount of the US traffic was transferred to Caernarvon, although the Canadian business was still routed through Clifden which continued to operate profitably right up to its enforced closure in 1922. Indeed, a major programme of modernisation was embarked upon between 1918 and 1920, with the replacement of the wood by steel masts in the antenna system and – more importantly – the introduction of power thermionic valves in the transmitter to replace the rotary spark gap.

Notwithstanding these modifications, developments in electronics – especially valves – proceeded world-wide at an ever-increasing pace following the First World War, leading to further technical improvements in the overall wireless systems. This led to the obvious question as to whether the remote western Clifden station would continue to be viable in the long term, especially with the success of Caernarvon. Indeed, the Company announced the phasing out of the station early in 1922 (the signing of the Anglo-Irish Treaty in December 1921 is quite likely to have been a factor) but this caused such a furore that the matter was postponed. It was obvious that it was only a temporary reprieve and the Clifden station had already began to outlive its usefulness and would not operate for much longer.

The matter was abruptly resolved in July 1922, following the outbreak of the Irish Civil War in June, when the station was occupied by 'Irregular' Republican forces and, whilst not destroyed, suffered considerable damage to some of the installations, especially the condenser housing. The station was not recaptured by the National Army (Commander in-Chief, General Michael Collins) until 15 August. Some attempt was made by the new Irish Government to have repairs carried out but the Marconi Company only made a few token efforts.[8] The station lingered on until its final closure in 1925 when the equipment was sold off as scrap metal. This was an ignominious end to what had been, in its time, the most technically advanced wireless station in the world, with the perfection of the rotary spark gap and the directional antenna to its credit. It was second in size only to Marconi's major international installation at Coltano, near Livorno in Italy.

Thus Clifden went down the same path of destruction as Crookhaven in the same year. It was alleged that there was some secret protocol in the Anglo-Irish Treaty which would permit Britain to continue using the station for military purposes, and a similar excuse was given in the case of Crookhaven. As mentioned previously, there may have been some validity in the case of Crookhaven since the Royal Navy continued to use nearby Berehaven until 1938, but the nearest British base to Clifden in the Free State after 1921 was in Lough Swilly, Co. Donegal. In any case, I have never heard further reference to this alleged protocol in the treaty, and it does appear to have been a useful red herring whenever someone wanted to impute something underhand in the treaty negotiations – or worse, to make excuses for destroying the wireless stations at Clifden and Crookhaven. It must also be mentioned that up to 1,000 people in the Clifden area were affected financially by the abrupt closure arising from this single mindless act of political vandalism, leading to the emigrant ship once again.

---

8 For further discussion of the capture of the Marconi station at Clifden, cf. R. Pine, *2RN and the origins of Irish Radio* (Dublin: Four Courts Press, 2002) pp. 18-20 (the first volume in the series 'Broadcasting and Irish Society').

CHAPTER 9

Guglielmo Marconi and Beatrice O'Brien

From 1902 onwards, when it was obvious that wireless was about to be a permanent and expanding factor in communications, the inevitable and, of course, undignified scramble began for control of the new medium. Naturally, Marconi became the main object of attack and had to fend off criticisms of his successes not only from the Post Office and the Military but, in particular, from Adolph Slaby of German Telefunken, who was intent on usurping Marconi's successful commercial enterprises, especially following the astonishing transatlantic test in December 1901. It was obvious that, in all probability and sooner or later, Marconi would ultimately commercialise the transatlantic link which was a source of great alarm to the cable companies, since global long-distance wireless would be a major rival to the existing cable networks.

In the midst of all these aggressive interactions, Marconi, who was in a thorough state of disillusionment, fell in love. In 1904 he was thirty years old, famous, rich and single. He led a very active social life, enjoying sailing and driving up to London in his Mercedes (which was probably one of the few in England at that time) usually to be one of the honoured guests of fashionable receptions 'in town' or, if not London, attending elaborately organised Edwardian weekends in the country. He was certainly able to move effortlessly between business and social affairs. On one occasion when he was working in the makeshift laboratories at the Haven Hotel, he lunched with his friends the Van Raaltes who owned an island several miles away in Poole Harbour. On arrival at the island jetty by boat he was introduced to one of Mrs Van Raalte's young guests – Beatrice O'Brien, then aged nineteen.

Beatrice O'Brien, or Bea as she was affectionately known, was one of seven daughters of the 14th Baron Inchiquin, Edward Donagh O'Brien, and of his wife Ellen Harriett, who lived in Dromoland Castle, Co. Clare. One Italian text with typical flamboyance described the Inchiquins as being '*di famiglia nobilissima che avera additura tenuto la corona d'Irlande prima dell'occupazione elisabettina*' (a most noble family who had directly held the crown of Ireland before the Elizabethan occupation).[1] This presumably refers to the O'Briens' being descended from

---

1 A. Giacomelli and G. Bertocchi, *Guglielmo Marconi: Come Nasce un Genio: le origine montane e l'ascesa della famiglia* (Bologna: Nuèter-Ricerche, 1994), p. 188.

Figure 9.1 Marconi's first wife Beatrice O'Brien

King Brian Boru who was slain by the Vikings in his tent during the battle of Clontarf, near present day Dublin, in 1014.

Marconi was anything but an impulsive man, yet the moment that he saw Beatrice he knew that he wanted to marry this high-spirited Irish country girl who was incredibly beautiful, yet so naïve and so abominably dressed ('The dress she had on was *awful*' he always said – and it was the best one in Bea's wardrobe).

The O'Brien-Inchiquin world was astronomically remote from the world of Marconi in which he moved freely amongst rich, sophisticated and well-dressed women, who 'for some years now had thrown themselves (or their daughters) at his head and would for the rest of his life go on throwing themselves at him'. On the contrary, Bea's appearance was anything but smart, and she was noticeably ill-at-ease in Marconi's company, intimidated no doubt by his burgeoning fame and his thirty-year-old maturity. Nevertheless, Marconi continued to press his intentions and even mentioned that he was asking his (existing) fiancée to release him from his engagement On his return to London, literally following Bea, the chase continued and he proposed soon afterwards. Bea asked for some time to consider the matter and then turned him down.

With typical aplomb, Marconi treated his rejection as merely temporary and travelled to Turkey, Bulgaria and Romania, wearing his broken heart on his well-pressed sleeve. In these countries he proposed new wireless stations which he hoped would link all the corners of the earth. However, emotionally and physically depleted, he contracted malaria in the Balkans and the recurrent paroxysms of fever plagued him for years afterwards.

The broken romance was renewed when Marconi contrived to visit the island off Poole again in late 1904, and this time the courtship was successful and Bea accepted his proposal, subject to family approval which was not forthcoming initially, the main objector being Lady Inchiquin herself. After all, although a Protestant, Marconi was a foreigner, albeit only 50 per cent since his mother was a Jameson. Moreover, rumours were circulating that he had been seen in the company of an Italian princess and had been previously engaged. At this stage Bea was inconsolable, but Marconi rushed back to London, shortening a business trip, and brought the smile back to Bea's expression. It was also clear that he had impressed the family by the speed with which he had come to her side. When he added his charm, reasonableness and elegant manner (after all, he was a 'gentleman'), the O'Brien family capitulated 'en masse' and the engagement was announced in the Court Circular.

Bea herself was almost overcome by the sudden change in the attitude of her family, but they had finally realized that Marconi was a very good 'catch' and that he was accepted, even lionised, by society, being welcomed equally in Mayfair, Fifth Avenue or the Quirinal, followed everywhere by the press. Although marriage to a 'titled gentleman' was every mother's dream for her daughters, Marconi was universally considered to be an outstanding second best (in fact he acquired the title of 'Marchese' in Italy during the 1920s). Furthermore, notwithstanding his genuine worries about the financial state of his company, in terms of personal income he was comfortably well-off, came from rich families on both sides and, of course, was expected to become even richer. All this may have been of some interest to the relatively impoverished Inchiquins.

The wedding took place in St George's Church, Hanover Place, on 16 March 1905, then as now one of the most fashionable churches in London. The bride, accompanied by her brother Lucius, arrived by coach (borrowed). When they arrived they were astonished, if not appalled that, in addition to royalty and other guests, the general public had also chosen to attend. Across the city of London on that day, headlines appeared on the billboards: MARCONI TO WED DAUGHTER OF IRISH PEER. Hanover Square was crowded.

Two days before the wedding, a potentially black cloud had appeared above the general preamble in the form of a semi-illiterate letter stating that the bridegroom would be assassinated – no person or organisation was specified. On the actual day, two relations of Bea, together with detectives, were situated near the church portals, scanning the invitees for anyone who looked suspicious. Unless the would-be assassin was elegantly and expensively dressed – which was not likely – it was doubtful if he could get anywhere near the entrance. In the event, no bombs exploded, or shots were fired, but the anxious Lucius ensured that Bea and himself arrived at the church a full half-hour before the ceremony, much to her chagrin, since Marconi did not arrive until after her.

Amongst the vast array of presents received – silver, jewels, lace, plates and glasses enough for banquets – was a particularly significant gift from Alexander Popov himself who sent a sealskin coat and a silver samovar from St Petersburg. Popov had designed and successfully tested a wireless receiver almost identical with that of Marconi in 1895 and considerable controversy persisted subsequently for over fifty years regarding the credit for being first in the field of wireless. Marconi is now generally accepted as *the* pioneer since, although the dates were more or less synchronised (bearing in mind the old Tsarist calendar), Popov had confined his studies to *reception* of thunderstorms only, whereas Marconi developed a complete transmitter-receiver and subsequently commercialised it at Ballycastle. Popov's gift was all the more poignant since he died later in the same year of 1905.

The honeymoon in the ancient seat of the Inchiquins at Dromoland Castle, Co. Clare was offered to the newlyweds by Bea's brother Lucius. At this stage the castle was virtually empty and Bea herself found it quite depressing compared with her childhood days. As for her husband, he was almost frozen with the cold and draughts and the whole stay was an unmitigated disaster. In addition, Marconi took to taking day walks on his own and this of course compounded Bea's misery. Fortunately the honeymoon came to a premature end after only one week because Marconi's presence in England was needed for urgent business. There is little doubt that both were happier in the less constricting atmosphere of London.

Bea now found herself in a world completely different from Dromoland which she had shared with six brothers and six other sisters plus a multitude of transient visitors of their own ages. It turned out that Marconi was a singularly undomesticated man and, at this particular period of relentless work and travel, simply did not have the time or inclination to involve himself in domestic affairs. With the transatlantic development involving Clifden and Glace Bay in full swing, constant liner trips to and from North America – on some of which Bea accompanied him – enduring the privations of the harsh Canadian winter, and living in a two-bedroom house – obviously placed some strain on the newly-weds. Furthermore their first child, born in February 1906, died after some weeks, leaving Bea distraught and Guglielmo disconsolate.

Bea always enjoyed herself in London where the couple had a town house and, later, a country residence in Hampshire. She enjoyed herself even more in Italy, both at the Villa Griffone with Marconi's mother Annie and with the café society in Rome. Then, in September 1908, their daughter Degna was born, but Marconi was abroad at the time which, if only temporarily, led to ominous strains between the couple.

Figure 9.2 Marconi with his first family. From left, Degna, Beatrice O'Brien, Gioia and (standing) Giulio

The interminable trips went on relentlessly and when Marconi went to America, Bea stayed at home with Degna. Then she discovered that she was pregnant again and, hoping that the next arrival would be a boy, she was determined to tell her husband personally as soon as possible. Since Marconi was on the high seas, a 'Marconigram' to the liner approaching Ireland would appear to be the obvious method of giving him the good news. Instead Bea chose a more spectacular way. She crossed to Ireland and at Queenstown (Cobh), in Cork harbour, succeeded in getting aboard a tugboat that was just departing to meet the liner which was then in the outer harbour and in which her husband was a passenger. His astonished welcome, when Bea appeared out of the sea like a mermaid, bore no trace of the ecstasy that she expected. In fact Marconi had temporarily returned to his bachelor days and was the centrepiece of a party on board which included Enrico Caruso, flushed with success after performances at the New York Metropolitan Opera, together with more than one enchantress from the operatic world. Bea realised that she was intruding and retired to her husband's cabin in an extremely tearful state.[2]

---

2 Degna Marconi, *My Father Marconi*, pp 181ff.

The next morning Marconi, covered in shame, apologised abjectly and even implored her to join the party. But Bea obviously felt that this was only adding insult to injury and flatly refused, emerging only when the ship finally docked at Liverpool. This had been a serious affair between two proud, hot-tempered and quick-tongued people and the coolness between them persisted for several months, with Bea only thawing out in December 1909 when they both travelled to Stockholm together where Marconi received the Nobel prize for Physics along with Braun of Telefunken.

The next arrival on the family scene actually was a boy christened Giulio and born in May 1910. Bea's fervent wish had come true. Again Marconi was absent for the birth but did send a telegram. The family was completed with the arrival of a second girl, Gioia, in April 1916 in London at the height of the First World War with German Zeppelins flying overhead. Marconi was a military attaché in the Italian Embassy at the time. It will be recalled that Italy took the side of the allies during that war against the central powers, mainly consisting of Austria-Hungary and Germany.

It will be clear at this stage that all was not well in the Marconi household, which seemed to be racked with dissension from time to time, accentuated by the frequent travel of Marconi and constant moving about in hotels and residences. This appeared to worsen with time, and even the intervention of mutual friends failed to heal the serious rift between Bea and Guglielmo. In fact there appeared to be only one inevitable outcome.

CHAPTER 10

Guglielmo Marconi – patron of the arts

Apart from his professional activities involving wireless telegraphy, Marconi also had a genuine interest in cultural affairs. He probably inherited his love of music, especially singing, from his mother Annie Jameson who, as a young girl, had studied at the Conservatorio Musicale in Bologna.

Marconi visited London frequently for long periods and was to be seen regularly at the many musical events, opera, theatre and soirées in various residences of London society. During the 1920s he was the Chairman of the Royal Society of Arts which, although interpreting 'Arts' in the broad sense, was a very prestigious institution.

In 1916, in the middle of the war that was tearing mainland Europe apart and with the Easter Rebellion breaking out in Ireland, Marconi was a military attaché at the Italian Embassy in London liaising in the field of wireless telegraphy with British colleagues, as wireless was now being used on a large scale by both sets of protagonists.[1] One evening at a reception to which Marconi had been invited by a wealthy London philanthropist, Lord Howard de Walden, Marconi was astonished to hear the extraordinary youthful singing of a beautiful Irish girl, Margaret Burke Sheridan, then training in London for an operatic career. He actually sought her out after the performance exclaiming, 'This is the voice I have waited to hear all my life'. Just who was Margaret Burke Sheridan?

Margaret Sheridan was born in Castlebar, Co. Mayo, in October 1889, the fifth surviving child of the local postmaster John Burke Sheridan and his wife Mary Ellen. In fact John Sheridan was a descendant of the famous playwright and member of Parliament, Richard Brinsley Sheridan. The family background

---

1 Unlike the Second World War, Italy took the side of the western allies in the First World War, declaring war on the Central Powers in 1915, its main preoccupation being the major threat on its northern frontier from Austro-Hungary which, of course, was determined to restore the Po valley to the Hapsburg empire. Following his stay in London, Marconi was posted to the Italian northern front in 1917, where he participated in the battle of Caporetto which Italians refer to as the 'Somme of the Southern Front', suffering huge losses and being all but routed. The Austro-Hungarians actually managed to push the Italian armies into Italy itself but were stopped again with enormous losses on both sides, the Italians holding out until the Armistice in 1918. Italy, in fact, broke the Hapsburg empire's southern flank and to this day still resents the fact that, notwithstanding the huge price paid in the battles, no significant territorial rewards were forthcoming at the Treaty of Versailles. Indeed, this may have been a factor in its entering the Second World War on the German side, but, of course, Mussolini was the prime mover in this decision.

Figure 10.1 Marconi as a military attaché during World War I

was stable and Margaret started life in a very pleasant environment, especially as her parents were very popular in the town and the position of postmaster gave her father some status. At that time, there was considerable political activity with demands for Home Rule within the framework of constitutional nationalism, but also an increasing level of violence, especially in the countryside where evictions were becoming commonplace and 'landlordism' was a hated word. The colossal figures of Charles Parnell and Michael Davitt (who was a Mayoman) immediately come to mind. The Sheridans would most probably have remained relatively untouched in Castlebar and the initial years of Margaret's life seemed secure and serene.

On 25 April 1895 Margaret's mother died at the age of forty-two following complications resulting from acute influenza. The totally unexpected loss of her mother to whom, as the youngest, she was deeply attached, was a frightening and traumatic experience for her at the tender age of five. But worse was to follow, as her father began to have serious parental difficulties with his eldest son, from whom he ultimately became completely estranged His health began to suffer under the strain, and he eventually died in February 1901. Margaret was now an orphan at the age of eleven, but she was not exactly the penniless orphan dependent on the charity of others as was luridly painted by the media of later years. As mentioned in the excellent biography by Anne Chambers, Margaret's father had made provisions for her in his will, by arranging to have the family house sold after his death. He also arranged to send her to the Dominican Convent in Dublin as a boarder for further education.[2]

Music was a specialty in this school and Margaret's talents as a future mezzo soprano were soon recognised both inside and outside the convent school, especially by Mother Clement who recognised Margaret's potential and personally supervised her initial training. It was obvious that further voice training would be very desirable, if not essential, to further her career and she was delighted to be accepted as a pupil by the Royal Academy of Music in London in 1909, financed by means of a special concert held in her honour in Dublin before her departure.

Also during this time in Dublin, Margaret was taught by Dr Vincent O'Brien, who had been a very active organist in church music and director of the Palestrina Choir of the Pro-Cathedral since 1903. John McCormack had been another of his more famous pupils. Dr O'Brien was subsequently appointed as the first musical director of the then-recently commissioned 2RN (Dublin) wireless station, later called Radio Éireann.[3]

---

2 Anne Chambers, *Margaret Sheridan, Irish Prima Donna* (Dublin: Wolfhound Press, 1989). 3 For O'Brien's career as Music Director of 2RN/Radio Éireann, see R. Pine, *2RN* chapter 5, passim and *Music and broadcasting* (Dublin: Four Courts Press, forthcoming) chapter 2, passim (also in the series 'Broadcasting and Irish Society').

Figure 10.2 Margaret Sheridan at the height of her London fame

Soon after arriving in London and having settled in at the Royal Academy, Margaret was fortunate to be befriended by Olga Lind, a famous teacher, and through her she met many influential people including Lord Howard de Walden. Following his astonishing opening remark, Marconi told her what she already knew: that she had fulfilled her potential in England and that only in Italy, the land of *bel canto*, could her full ambition be developed. In fact, Marconi offered her the opportunity to go to Italy under his protection and patronage. Margaret was now in a major quandary, since she was all but betrothed to Richard Hazelton, a dashing young 35-year-old Irish Nationalist member of Parliament for Galway, and she had to decide between the love she needed and the career she desired. Eventually she chose the latter and accepted Marconi's offer. Although there is some belief that Lord de Walden was also involved in the financial arrangements and had known Margaret for some time, there is no doubt that Marconi was the prime mover in this most generous gesture.

Early in 1916, in the midst of the war-time chaos in Europe, Margaret and Marconi made their perilous way across the German submarine-infested English Channel and then proceeded by a tortuous train route for several weeks until they reached Milan on a bright and sunny day. Margaret's first impression of Italy was very positive indeed and she was even more impressed by Rome, where Marconi installed her in a first-class hotel on the famous Via Veneto.

Following the usual round of much sought-after recitals in the palazzi of the Roman society, Marconi personally arranged to have Margaret study under the operatic teacher and conductor Alfredo Martino, who raised her tone from mezzo to full soprano. Margaret was expected to stay in Italy for six months but, as things turned out, the months stretched into years and, during her study period with Martino, she met many of the great names of Italian opera: Boito, Giordano, Mascagni, Battistino, Ruffo and, some time later, Gigli.

At that time the impresario of the Rome opera was Emma Carelli who, in her day, had been a well-known soprano. Faced with a crisis on her hands arising from the sudden illness of her leading soprano, she approached Margaret who, at four days' notice, agreed to take on the role of Mimi in *La bohème*, much to the dismay of Signor Martino, who did not consider her yet sufficiently trained to take on this exacting role. Sadly, he was proved to be ultimately correct in this assessment. Margaret's performance was absolutely masterly and after she had sung the first few notes she had this large, distinguished and very critical audience in the palm of her hand and her career in Italy was assured. Puccini himself considered her to be the perfect Mimi and the only Butterfly.

Margaret next made her début at the famous La Scala, Milan, and became so completely identified with the part of 'Butterfly' that she was frequently called by that name in the streets. Another name popular with the media of the time was 'The Irish Nightingale'. This was indeed a far cry from 'Maggie from Mayo' with which title she once styled herself in a memorable broadcast from Radio Éireann. Margaret's meteoric career was now in full swing, and her début at Covent Garden occurred in 1919, with what was now the anticipated total audience success and, of course, her actual range of operas was increasing all the time with works from Mascagni, Boito, Catalani, Respighi, Giordano and Verdi in addition to Puccini.[4] She had a singular success in 1930 when Gigli chose her to sing with him at Covent Garden. It should be added that performances were also given by her in Germany, France and the USA.

However, some ominous health problems began to surface in the form of nose and throat difficulties as early as 1926. These became progressively more frequent and forced Margaret to cancel several important engagements, leading inevitably to a lack of confidence. Furthermore, relations between herself and her long-time friend Eustace Blois, Managing Director at Covent Garden, became more distant with time. These two factors eventually led Margaret to abandon singing altogether in 1934 to the consternation of her friends and she remained absolutely adamant about this. There was little doubt, however, that her ability to sing the high Bs and Cs had almost abandoned her, and the interruption of her training with Maestro Martino to sing – against his express wishes – in *La bohème* at the persistent request of Emma Carelli in 1918 was now taking its toll. It might be remarked that Margaret was reaping the bitter harvest of a late beginning, coupled with inadequate preparation.[5]

Having successfully guided her initially, Marconi had taken a discreet back seat and observed the progress of his protegée from afar, no doubt taking immense satisfaction in having established 'Maggie from Mayo' as a major international operatic soprano. Obviously it cost a considerable sum of money to bring her career to fruition, and without his assistance and encouragement it is unlikely Margaret could have progressed right to the top. Recalling Marconi's own strong Irish background, it is more than probable that altruism played a part in his decision to assist this talented Irish lady towards an extraordinary career, which brought her from one of the remotest parts of Western Europe to the heady sophistication of Rome.

4 Liam Breen, *HMV Treasury* EMI Archives HLM 7076, 1975. **5** Margaret Sheridan finally retired to Ireland in 1937 and died in 1958 after a long and painful illness. She is buried in Glasnevin, Dublin.

CHAPTER 11

Further activities of Marconi
in Ireland, 1922–37

The 1916 wireless broadcast in Ireland

> 1916 was the year of the Irish Easter rebellion and the first radio broadcast (in Europe). The Irish rebels used a ships wireless to make not a point-to-point message, but a diffused broadcast in the hope of getting word to some ships that would relay their story to the American press. And so it proved.
>
> Marshal McLuhan[1]

Easter Monday, 24 April 1916, saw the outbreak of what became known in certain quarters as the 'Sinn Féin Rebellion'. The GPO in Sackville (now O'Connell) Street was the command post and a complete ship's wireless was set up on the roof of an adjoining building from which the Morse code on the shipping wavelength was used for the broadcasting.[2]

There is no record of any reception of the broadcast which was continuously repeated for about one day. The authorities had succeeded in putting Clifden off the air, but news of the rebellion was in fact sent from the Marconi station at Valentia and appeared in American newspapers.

As referred to in detail by Richard Pine, the actual broadcast led to several conflicting opinions over the years because of its blatant illegality – which was hardly a priority with the republicans. In particular Conor Cruise O'Brien wrote 'like most war propaganda it was designedly inaccurate and misleading ... The painful conclusion is, I think, inescapable ... Broadcasting was conceived in sin. It is a child of wrath. There is no knowing what it may not yet get up to'.[3]

R.J. Levey, referring specifically to McLuhan's comment, states: 'Such a broadcast may well have been a "first" but its real significance was perhaps not that attributed to it by McLuhan. More importantly, it was the first known

---

1 M. McLuhan, *Understanding Media* (London: Routledge, 2001 repr.); the first wireless broadcast was actually in the USA in 1906 by J.S. Fessenden who transmitted *music* to a ship 10 miles from the shore. He used a HF generator as the carrier frequency and like many of Fessenden's achievements this has largely been forgotten. **2** R. Pine, *2RN*, pp 10–11. **3** C.C. O'Brien, Symposium on direct satellite broadcasting, Dublin 1977, European Space Agency/European Broadcasting Union.

deliberate misuse of wireless broadcasting and a sad precedent for the decades to come.'[4]

On the other hand Maurice Gorham states without equivocation, 'Whether or not the broadcasts reached their destination it showed great imagination for the men who planned the Rising to think of using wireless for such a purpose as early as 1916 (James Connolly is credited as the prime mover). They were, of course, ahead of their time.'[5]

It may sound somewhat bizarre to place such emphasis on legality, but it should be recalled that both O'Brien, who was Minister for Posts and Telegraphs at the time, and Levey were surveying the presence of countless 'pirate' radio and television stations in many countries (and offshore) in the late 1970s with consequent pollution of the airwaves. In some countries, Italy in particular, the stations were euphemistically termed 'private' instead of pirate.

First public broadcast in Ireland: Marconi's first transmission
Marconi was extremely upset regarding the virtual destruction of the Clifden station[6] but by this stage (1922–3) he had turned his attention to broadcasting and was already involved with the BBC. Ireland also figured in his plans and in August 1923, engineers from Marconi's Wireless Co. (UK) installed a low power transmitter in the main tower of the Royal Marine Hotel, Dún Laoghaire. The object of the test was to send selected transmissions to the grounds of the Royal Dublin Society which was about four miles distant.

The experiment was a complete success, with live music recitals being received clearly on crystal receivers and, even more intriguing, broadcast relays from stations in Newcastle and Manchester. However, after several days the Irish Postmaster-General abruptly withdrew permission for the test and asked the Marconi engineers to remove all the equipment – which was done immediately. There was some controversy at the time about the reason for this – one theory being that the Irish Government became concerned that the Marconi Company would obtain a monopoly on broadcasting in much the same manner as it had in England at this stage. However, the destruction of the Clifden and Crookhaven stations would have been recalled during these tests, yielding a basic sympathy for Marconi and the State did ultimately reward him when the state-controlled Irish Broadcasting Service was finally introduced some years later.

The beginning of public service broadcasting: Marconi transmitters in Ireland
It was obvious that public interest was increasing significantly regarding the possibility of broadcasting in Ireland, especially since the BBC commenced transmissions in November 1922, some of which were received clearly in

4 R.J. Levey, 'A century of trust in Mother Nature', *EBU Technical Review* 263, 1995. 5 M. Gorham, *Forty Years of Irish Broadcasting* (Dublin: Talbot Press, 1967). 6 P. Clarke, *Dublin Calling: 2RN and the Birth of Irish Radio* (Dublin: RTÉ, 1986).

Figure 11.1 Irish Radio and Musical Review, vol. 2, no. 4, 1927

Ireland. However, the unstable political situation following the Treaty signing in December 1921, and the gradual slide towards outright civil war which broke out in June 1922, meant that the Government had no option but to postpone any decision on the future of broadcasting.

By that time there were several firm enquiries on the table, viz., Marconi's Wireless Telegraph Company, the *Daily Express* newspaper, Siemens Berlin and Uebersee Handel, also from Berlin. It should be remarked that newspapers were becoming somewhat anxious about news competition from broadcasters, which may explain the *Daily Express* interest.

Wireless broadcasting and listening received a major boost in the northern part of the now partitioned island when a low power (1.5kw) station commenced operations in September 1924. This received massive publicity in Belfast with Lord Abercorn, Governor of Northern Ireland, J.C. Reith (Managing Director of the BBC) and P.P. Eckersley (Chief Engineer of the BBC) present at the opening. A feature of the transmitter was that the aerial wire was suspended between two chimneys in a power station almost 200ft in height.

Notwithstanding the ruinous state of the country after the Civil War which ended in May 1923, the Free State Government actually presented a White Paper to the Dáil as early as September 1923 with a proposal for a broadcasting system. A Special Dáil Committee was appointed, and after three Interim Reports produced its final version in March 1924. The usual debates in the Dáil and Seanad then followed, which make interesting if not amusing reading (*plus ça change*) and finally in June 1925, the Minister for Finance approved expenditure for a broadcast service to be run by the Post Office.[7] A station was to be located in Dublin with another to follow in Cork. Work began immediately and a Marconi 1.5kw transmitter (Call Sign '2RN') was situated in McKee Barracks near Phoenix Park in Dublin with the studio and offices near the GPO off Henry Street. The studio was finally located in the GPO itself until the new Radio and Television Centre was set up in Donnybrook, in the 1960s.

The Cork Station ('6CK') commenced transmitting in 1927 and, effectively following the central location of Daventry in England, a powerful 100kw station began operations from near Athlone in February 1933.

The Marconi Company supplied the transmitters for all three stations and it is ironic that, a mere three years after the destruction of the gigantic transatlantic Clifden station, Guglielmo Marconi was 'back in business' in the newly emerged Irish Free State. It is also a tribute to the Government and engineers of the time who, although beset by major problems on all sides arising from the Civil War, were able and willing to initiate such a successful venture.

However, it is possible and more than likely that altruism was not the only factor in establishing the broadcasting stations. The hard and unpalatable (to some) fact was that the country was virtually saturated on the east and south coasts, together with the border counties, by the BBC which, by 1927, was almost five years in operation. It behoved the new state to assert itself with its

---

7 Cf. R. Pine, *2RN passim.*

Figure 11.2 The original Marconi transmitter in Athlone, 1934: the control room, with Mr Alex Gibbons at the central desk

own broadcasting system, not only to counteract the BBC – naturally considered to be a 'pagan' station in fundamentalist circles – but also to let the world know that the Irish Free State had arrived and was functioning.

International activities of Marconi, 1920–37
The Marconi domestic scene continued to be a turbulent affair until, finally, his marriage to Beatrice O'Brien was annulled in an amicable manner by a court in Fiume (now Rijeka, Croatia) in February 1924. Bea herself had become an Italian citizen at this stage and subsequently married the Marchese Marignoli di Spoleto, from the province of Umbria, in 1925.

In June 1927, Marconi married Maria Cristina Bezzi Scali of an old aristocratic family from the Ravenna-Bologna region and which was closely associated at a high level with papal affairs in the Vatican. This wedding took place in Rome and a daughter, Elettra, was born in 1930.

Marconi was now definitely moving in Italian high society, and in 1928 became President of the newly created National Council for Research (*Consiglio Nazionale delle Ricerche*, CNR) and also President of the Royal Italian Academy (*Reale Accademia d'Italia*), a position that automatically made him a member of the Grand Fascist Council. This placed him at the summit of political as well as academic influence. In the same year he was created a *marchese*.

Figure 11.3 Marconi and his wife Maria Cristina with their daughter Elettra
before a private audience with Pope Pius XI in 1934

It might be thought that this somewhat breathtaking list of record distinctions bestowed on Marconi by Benito Mussolini would have taken up so much time and effort that his major wireless interests would be relegated almost to the background. In fact, the reverse actually happened as illustrated by the major innovations in radio engineering at international level conducted by Marconi until his death in 1937.

In 1919, Marconi had successfully transmitted a telephone conversation from Ballybunion, Co. Kerry, to Louisville, Nova Scotia, following the introduction of thermionic valves. In turn this led to an experimental 15kw transmitter at the Marconi facility in Chelmsford from which Dame Nellie Melba broadcast her famous song recital in June 1920. Further music broadcasts followed, to the delight of wireless amateurs with their crystal set receivers. A further radio station commenced operations in London in May 1922, but complaints of interference with aircraft and other communication systems increased to such an extent that the Postmaster-General imposed strict licenses but also – and more importantly – asked the Marconi Company and five other large companies to form the British Broadcasting Company in 1922, subsequently renamed the British Broadcasting Corporation in 1926.

Wider coverage was soon required, and this led to the inauguration at Daventry, in 1924, of the high power longwave station now known as BBC Radio 4 operating at 198kHz (1500m).

The year 1924 marked the beginning of the shortwave era, when Appleton demonstrated the existence of the ionosphere by means of pulses reflected back to earth. The 1902 prediction of Heaviside, following Marconi's famous experiment across the Atlantic in 1901, was thus verified in a striking manner. Marconi had thought that shortwaves could only travel over short distances and, as we know, concentrated on long waves which required the gigantic aerial systems at Poldhu, Clifden, Caernarvon and Glace Bay. Appleton's discovery changed everything, and Marconi, along with his engineer R.N. Franklin, was the first to exploit 'Skywave propagation' via the ionosphere when he succeeded in transmitting signals over a distance of 4000km in 1924. Comparison with the 'traditional' longwave transmissions from Caernarvon showed that a transmitter power 100 times greater was needed for a reception similar to the shortwaves.

Using his yacht *Elettra*, which was really a floating laboratory, Marconi virtually surveyed the whole world by sea, and his success was such that he obtained a contract from the British Post Office to establish a shortwave system connecting Britain directly with its Commonwealth countries. The world-wide cable system of Julius Reuter sixty years previously was in the process of being replaced.

At this stage there was immense and insatiable enthusiasm amongst the general public for broadcasting, and in order to satisfy demands on a world-wide

Figure 11.4 Marconi's yacht *Elettra* in Genoa harbour, 1930

basis, the BBC commissioned Marconi to build a shortwave transmitter at Chelmsford. Thus in 1932 transmissions began from what is now known as the BBC World Service. (The original title of the BBC *Empire* Service is hardly relevant today.)

Marconi's research interests next extended to even shorter wavelengths, e.g. 0.5-metre (about 600MHz) and he realised that parabolic reflectors of manageable dimensions could give directional radiated power. His first venture was a microwave telephone link between Vatican City and the papal summer residence at Castelgandolfo in the Alban hills, ten kilometres from Rome. The fact that his father-in-law was a Papal Count may have had some influence in the awarding of the contract.

Marconi's most spectacular and dramatic public demonstration also proved to be his last. In 1934 he arranged for his yacht *Elettra*, with its windows blacked out, to steam into the harbour of Sestri Levante, near La Spezia on the Ligurian coast, guided by a microwave beacon which he had installed on neighbouring cliffs. The ship sailed effortlessly between two buoys at the mouth of the

Figure 11.5 The 'floating radio' laboratory on board the *Elettra*

harbour. One of the most interesting and unexpected results was that a hissing noise was heard in the receiver whenever another ship or a car passed through the beam. This was probably the first demonstration of radar, and coincided with the research then beginning in Britain which led to the military radar systems of the Second World War.

In the late 1920s Marconi's heart began to give trouble in the form of angina, but it did not prevent him from undertaking a world tour during 1933–4, when he visited the United States, Japan and China, being entertained royally everywhere. He suffered two severe heart attacks at the end of 1934 but recovered. Then Mussolini asked him to travel abroad again, in 1935, as a roving ambassador seeking to justify the Italian invasion of Ethiopia in 1935 which had caused consternation in the League of Nations in Geneva of which Éamon de Valera was President at the time. A key factor of Marconi's worldwide mission was to broadcast in each of the countries visited. This included the United States (twice). However, he was publicly rebuffed by the BBC in November 1935. Although Marconi subsequently personally pressed his request with Sir John Reith, the Director-General of the Corporation, the latter adhered to his original negative decision. At this stage Marconi was clearly becoming disillusioned with the Fascist regime and felt that Mussolini would listen only to what he wanted to hear. However, he undertook another exhausting tour which

Figure 11.6 The *Elettra* at the moment when Marconi led the ship between two buoys, using his 'blind navigation' (*navigazione cieca*) near the harbour of Sestri Levante in the Ligurian Sea, 1933–4

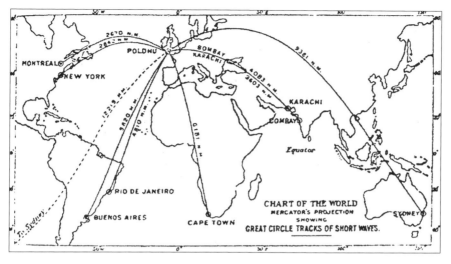

Figure 11.7 The Imperial Wireless Chain system which linked the United Kingdom
with its overseas dominions by means of a shortwave radio network developed by
the Marconi Company, beginning in 1926

proved to be his last, as he became progressively more ill on his return and died
on 20 July 1937.

A two-minute silence of wireless stations throughout the world was observed
as a fitting tribute to his massive contribution in conquering the airwaves and the
name of Marconi will be forever linked not just to radio itself but to all the subsequent developments in that area, now ranging from digital satellite
communications to information technology.

Concluding remarks
As regards Ireland, it is clear that Marconi not only had a far greater involvement
than has usually been acknowledged, but also carried out some of his pioneering
work in Ireland – for example: the commercial link between Ballycastle and
Rathlin Island, Kingstown Regatta reporting for marine communications, the
reception at Crookhaven from Poldhu, strongly indicating that a transatlantic
wireless link seemed possible (as it was), and finally the transatlantic wireless
telephone from Ballybunion.

Even after the destruction of the Crookhaven and Clifden stations and the
aftermath of the Civil War, Marconi turned his attention to broadcasting stations
in Ireland and provided the transmitters for Dublin and subsequently Cork and
Athlone. The Athlone station was installed only four years before his death in
1937. As has been mentioned several times in the text, Marconi's Irish connec-

Figure 11.8 Guglielmo Marconi and Benito Mussolini on board the *Elettra*, 1930

tions through his mother Annie Jameson and his wife of nineteen years, Beatrice O'Brien, undoubtedly influenced him throughout most of his life for the overall benefit to this country, especially in his latter years when Ireland was struggling towards nationhood and recognition after a singularly inauspicious beginning.[8]

8 The following references will supplement the information in this chapter: G. Marconi, 'radio communi-cations', *Journal of the Royal Society of Arts*, 26 December 1924; G. Marconi, 'Radio communications by means of very short waves', *Proceedings of the Royal Institution of Great Britain*, vol. 22, 1933; G. Marconi, *Scritti di Guglielmo Marconi Reale Accademia d'Italia*, 1941; E.H. Armstrong, 'The spirit of discovery: an appreciation of the work of Marconi', American Institute of Electrical Engineers Meeting, Atlantic City N.J., June 15-19, 1953; A.H. Beck, *Words and Waves* (London: Weidenfeld and Nicholson, 1967); A. Guagnini and G. Pancaldi, *Cento Anni di Radio: Le Radici dell'Invenzione* (Turin: SEAT, 1995); R.W. Burns (ed.), *100 Years of Radio*, IEE Conference Publication No.411, 1995; G.T. Waters (ed.) 'A century of wireless', *European Broadcasting Union Technical Review*, Spring 1995.

Marconi centenary celebrations in Ireland

The direct link between Ireland and the Marconi family took on a new and different lease of life in June 1994, when Princess Elettra, Marconi's youngest daughter, by his second marriage to Cristina Bezzi-Scali, arrived in Ireland, together with the President of the Fondazione Guglielmo Marconi, Professor Gian Carlo Corazza. In addition, a delegation of fifteen arrived from Bologna itself, representing various relevant elements of the city, councillors, journalists, educationalists, etc.

The highlight of the visit was the organising of the Round Table Discussion by RTÉ, in association with the Istituto Italiano di Cultura, Dublin, mainly concerned with various aspects of the consequences of Marconi's great invention 100 years ago with emphasis on his involvement in Ireland. A replica of the first

Figure 12.1 Princess Elettra Marconi speaking at the 1994 Marconi seminar in Dublin.

Figure 12.2 Marconi, with one of his co-directors, Godfrey Isaacs, demonstrating a car radio telephone in the late 1920s. This is possibly the first test of a mobile phone.

Marconi spark transmitter was actually fabricated by Mr Paddy Clarke of RTÉ specifically for the celebration.

In June 1995 a major gathering took place in Clifden in the presence of Princess Elettra, who unveiled a plaque at the site of the wireless station at Derrygimla, which was followed by lectures both in Clifden and Galway. The Italian Navy also participated on this occasion, recalling Marconi's naval involvement.

Finally in June 1998, Princess Elettra, who clearly has a strong attachment to Ireland, returned again to visit and unveil commemorative plaques at the extreme ends of Ireland, namely Ballycastle, Co. Antrim, and Crookhaven, Co. Cork.

'The meaning and possibilities of wireless telegraphy' by Professor Fitzgerald

Article by Professor G.F. Fitzgerald in the *Dublin Evening Mail* on 21 July 1898 in connection with the wireless reporting of the Kingstown Regatta (Chapter 4). It explains with extraordinary clarity the scientific basis of 'electromagnetic transmission without wires' which, of course, was a complete mystery to virtually every reader of the newspaper at that time.

On Tuesday last I had a most interesting experience. By the kindness of the *Daily Express* I was taken out on the steamer *Flying Huntress* and witnessed the first use of Wireless Telegraphy for newspaper reporting. The news conveyed on this occasion was for the information sent and not for the scientific knowledge of those sending it. The manoeuvres of the yachts were the sole object. The experiment was in every way completely successful. I am speaking now as an experimental philosopher constantly on the look out for further knowledge. The ability to make contact with the yachts in any weather and not just on a clear day was an unheard of experience until last Tuesday. On a more serious note the ability of the Kish lightship to communicate with the shore has obvious implications for safety at sea and, by extension, all the lightships and lighthouses around our coast would be able to give incalculable assistance to sailors in jeopardy. It is certainly far more important than transmissions for betting on yacht races. The mere fact of its commercial use in reporting proves its reliability and its possible extension in its present form to much greater things.

And what is the position now arrived at? Signor Marconi – to whom is due the actual advance from signalling to a distance of half a mile or so to signalling to a distance of tens of miles – and those who have worked at the subject know best how very great an advance this is – rigged up in a few days all the necessary apparatus on board the *Flying Huntress* and at Kingstown on shore, and immediately set to work, and sent signals to Kingstown from all over Dublin Bay and even from the far side of Howth, from places quite invisible from Killiney. Think what this means, in war, for instance, if, without laying telegraph wires, over hill and dale, in thick weather as in clear, bodies of troops and ships could communicate with one another. No doubt, an enemy might, in certain circumstances, either interfere with or read the signals. But so they can in any other known mode of communication, and yet nobody disputes the value of horse riders or carriers of despatches because they may be taken prisoners and their despatches read.

This Wireless Telegraphy has been looked upon as a thing that 'no fellah can understand.' It is to be regretted if the Dublin public think so. With his inimitable genius for exposition Mons. Molloy has brought the subject before them in lectures which 'every fellah' should understand. If they do not, it is one of the sins to be laid to the door of the Intermediate Board, who have been so eminently successful in their attempts to prevent our youth from studying science. Where Mons. Molloy has succeeded there is no use in attempting to make it clearer. Where he has failed it is useless for me to try. I may, however mention a few analogies to show those who think the whole subject mysterious that, after all, it is not so very far outside our other experience. In the first place, we are all probably familiar with the way in which a compass needle can be deflected by a magnet even though they are a distance apart with no wire or other apparent connexion between them. This turning of a compass needle by moving a magnet at a distance is an actual case of Wireless Telegraphy by magnetic influence. No doubt, the distance at which we can work successfully in this crude way is small, but it may be made quite considerable by means of very powerful magnets. It would require, however, very delicate apparatus and magnets on a very large scale, indeed, to work by this method to a distance of a mile and I doubt whether the *Flying Huntress* could carry the necessary magnets. I merely mention this case of 'wireless telegraphy' by magnetic influence to show that most people are familiar with an example of it, and thus to prevent them from looking upon the whole subject as some weird, incomprehensible thing beyond any ordinary human understanding. If anybody is not familiar with the way in which a magnet can move a compass needle when they are several inches apart, I would certainly advise their purchasing a small compass and magnet for a few pence and making the experiment for themselves, and they will see one of the most wonderful things in the whole world, and one the inner working of which is one of the problems that science is attacking at present with some prospect of success. 'But,' people will say, 'we are told that Wireless Telegraphy is accomplished by waves in the Ether.[1] There are no waves when I pull about a compass needle by moving a magnet.' That is quite true, and it will require another analogy to illustrate the difference.

Suppose people were all quite deaf: that they could no more perceive vibra-

1 The Ether (sometimes written as 'Aether') was thought to be a medium that was supposed to pervade all space and was 'invented' to explain the propagation of electromagnetic waves, e.g. light through space, since it was assumed that light could not propagate *in vacuo*. In 1898 the 'ether' theory was obviously believed by Fitzgerald. It was finally shown to be non-existent by Einstein in 1905 in the context of his Special Theory of Relativity.

tions of the air than they can in the ether that Signor Marconi uses, let us see how they might communicate with one another by means of the air. Well, they might blow light things about by means of fans. This would be like acting on the compass with the magnet. It would, of course, require enormously big fans to produce much effect at a hundred yards off. The effect of a fan spreads on all sides like the action of a magnet, and gets very feeble indeed at quite a short distance from the fan. It would be a great deal feebler when we went a hundred yards off than when we were one yard off, about a million times as feeble, and anybody who had tried to count a million will appreciate how very small this effect would be. It would be a great advance on this to use tubes to blow through. In fact, we might have tubes many miles long to blow through, and by means of blasts of air driven through the tubes blow light objects in or out of the tube at the far end, and thus signal to our friends at a distance. This would be like using electric currents which act on compass needles at a distant station to which telegraph wires lead the current. At this stage somebody might perchance invent a method of receiving air vibrations, sound waves, for which we each fortunately possess a most delicate receiving apparatus in our ears. At once people would be able to communicate by, for example, clapping their hands. The spark arrangement that Signor Marconi uses produces very much the same effect on the ether that clapping our hands does on the air, and his receiving apparatus receives the claps through the ether in a way dimly analogous to the way our ears receive the sound wave of a clap through the air. One might ask, Why is this any better than the fanning plan? Both of them produce a disturbance which rapidly diminishes in intensity by spreading abroad in every direction. No doubt; but the sound wave does not diminish at all so rapidly as the air current near the fan. At a hundred yards the sound would be only ten thousand times as faint as at one yard, instead of being a million times as faint, and, as I said before, those who have counted to ten thousand; and tried (for very few succeed) to count to a million will appreciate what a very great advance there is in using waves instead of simple currents in producing effects at a distance. It is quite unusual to signal to a distance by means of loud claps. Fog signals are frequently produced by gas explosions in fog guns; and there is an interesting analogy between them and Signor Marconi's arrangements. For example, if an observer near a fog-gun wanted to hear the fog signals from a passing ship he should be very careful to stop his own ears with cotton wool while his own gun was going off. His ears will otherwise be so disturbed by his own gun that they could not hear the fainter signals from a distance. Similarly Signor Marconi has boxed up his delicate receiving apparatus in a very satisfactory way, so that it may not be injured by the powerful ether explosions of his own signalling apparatus. Another hearing analogy illustrates another thing that is at first somewhat unintelligible, and that is, that the signalling is much more satisfactory at the Kish lightship than when close outside Kingstown Harbour. Anybody who tried to understand what another person says when bellowing into a telephone, or into one's ear, will understand how it requires a somewhat different adjustment, which, however, can be easily made, for near and far signalling.

The apparatus actually used cannot be described in sufficiently non-technical language to be worth describing in a public journal, but the salient part observable is worth mentioning. It consists of a long strip of ordinary galvanised iron wire netting hung from the top of the mast of the ship or from the mast onshore, and connected by an insulated wire with a Ruhmkorff coil. In the analogy of a fog-gun this wire net represents the gun, while the explosion of the gun is represented by the electric sparking of the Ruhmkorff coil. All these magnetic and electric actions are actions in the ether just as wind and sounds are due to actions in the air. Some people think of the ether as an unknowable assumption. There is every reason to believe that light, for example, takes 8 minutes to come from the sun, and it must exist en route, so that it is a vibration of something, that something must extend all the way to the sun. The ether is, then, a real something and, as a matter of fact, we know a great deal more about it than about air, and its properties are, so far as we know them, very much simpler that those of the air we are so familiar with. It propagates waves for Wireless Telegraphy at 182,000 miles per second, so that no hurricane in the air has any sensible effect on them; the velocity of the air of 100 miles an hour in a hurricane is far too slow to produce any effect upon the waves Signor Marconi uses. They are also unaffected by hail, rain, snow, or fog. This seems at first sight very remarkable. They are essentially the same as the light waves which are unaffected by wind, but which are seriously interfered with by other meteoric conditions, such as fog and dust. This, however, depends on the length of the waves. The waves of light are very short, quite small compared with the drop of rain or particles of water or dust suspended in a fog. The light waves are, however, large compared with the molecules of air itself, and can get among them quite freely. In the same way sounds are not seriously interfered by rain because they are very long compared with the rain drops. The waves Signor Marconi uses are probably a hundred yards long or thereabouts, and are consequently quite unaffected by meteoric conditions, and can go around large obstacles like mountains in the same way that sound waves can go around ordinary obstacles.

To anybody the experiences of last Tuesday would have been intensely interesting, but they are doubly so to those who appreciate that in them mankind had utilised the all-pervading ether as his servant, to carry his messages, and forged another link in the chain that harnesses lightening and thunder to the ear of human progress.

Geo. Fras. Fitzgerald.

The induction coil of
Nicholas Callan, 1836

The spectacular success of Marconi in transmitting the yachting results of the Kingstown Regatta across Dublin Bay in July 1898 has been outlined in Chapter 4. The spark gap transmitter used an induction coil designed and fabricated by Nicholas Callan, professor of Natural Philosophy at Maynooth.

Nicholas Callan (1799–1864) independently developed the induction coil as early as 1836, well before Ruhmkorff in 1851 to whom it is usually attributed. Furthermore, Callan's announcement of the Principle of the Self-Induced Dynamo in 1838 preceded Werner Siemens by no less than twenty-nine years (1867). It also now appears that Callan had no serious contact with Faraday but had studied at length the self-inductive work of Joseph Henry at Princeton. Unfortunately, Callan's achievements tended to fade into obscurity after his death but no one challenged his priority of invention in his lifetime.[1]

After much experimentation linking various coils magnetically, Callan finally produced the induction coil shown here in the original 1836 diagram in which the circuitry of a step-up transformer is immediately evident. This is, of course, a fundamental element in modern a/c electrical circuits and there is hardly an electrical/electronic device, both domestic and industrial, which does not include a transformer of some kind. Incidentally Callan's circuit owed nothing, precisely nothing, to Faraday's iron ring experiments. It is worth noting with near disbelief that both primary and secondary coils were successfully insulated by Callan using the famous viscous gutta-percha obtained from tropical trees which was subsequently used in the 1860s to insulate the transatlantic cables. Note the 1300ft of the secondary coil. The stepping up of the voltage would have been the order of volts in the primary rising to kilovolts in the secondary coil for the spark gap transmitter.

The 'H' in the figure represents – literally – shock *handles* which were sometimes gripped by unfortunate students as a detector. With similar circuits

---

1 M.C. Sexton. 'Early studies of electromagnetic and associated topics in Ireland', *Radio Science Bulletin* (URSI) 296, March 2001.

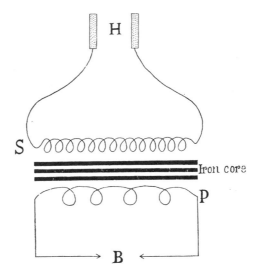

Figure A1 Schema of Callan Transformer with coils separated: *Ann. Elect. Mag. and Chem.* (Sturgeon), 1 (1836), 493; 2 (1837), 317; *Phil. Mag.* 9 (1836), 472. *B.* battery and contact breaker. *P.* primary coil, 50 feet of thick wire. *S.* secondary coil, 1,300 feet of thin wire.

Figure A2 The induction coil used by Marconi for the Kingstown Regatta in 1898. It is now in the Callan Museum at the National University of Ireland, Maynooth, Co. Kildare.

Callan successfully ignited the carbon in an arc lamp and 'electrocuted a large fowl'.[2] Callan, of course, was considered to be a somewhat eccentric genius by the clerical students at Maynooth which at that time was primarily a teaching college for the priesthood, especially after one student was knocked unconscious temporarily by high tension between the handles. For the record, this particular student was subsequently appointed Archbishop of Dublin.[3]

2 P.J. McLaughlin, 'Some Irish Contemporaries of Faraday and Henry', *Proceedings of the Royal Irish Academy* 64a/2, 17, September 1964. **3** P.J. McLaughlin, *Nicholas Callan, Priest-Scientist* (Dublin: Clonmore and Reynolds, 1965); C. Mallon and J. Upton, *The Scientific Apparatus of Nicholas Callan* (Dublin: Samton Press, 1994).

Comparison of inductive and radiative wireless transmissions (1897)

It is important to note that there are fundamental differences between electromagnetic induction and radiation. The original theory and experimentation of induction was developed by Ampère, Faraday and Henry between 1820 and 1840 and this has no connection with the electrodynamics portrayed by Maxwell in the 1860s and elegantly verified by Hertz in 1888.

Surprisingly, the failure on the part of several distinguished physicists to fully recognise this distinction led to some confusion and acrimony. The dimensions of the circuitry and the distance between transmitter and receiver compared to the electromagnetic wavelength determined whether the system was inductively or radiatively coupled.[1] In modern antenna theory induction links would be referred to as the 'near field' i.e. adjacent to the antenna, whereas radiation is associated with the 'far field' transmission. All communication links operate in the far field region.

The following paper published by W.H. Preece entitled *Signalling Through Space without Wires*, in 1897, also a discourse before the Royal Institution, gives an extremely comprehensive if not philosophical account of progress to that date, including comments on the non-existent 'ether'. A direct comparison is made, including circuitry, of Preece's own inductive method with the radiative experiments of Marconi (Chapter 4).

---

1 A.H.W. Beck, *Words and Waves*, op. cit. chapter 5.

With the Authors Compliments

SIGNALLING

THROUGH SPACE

WITHOUT WIRES.

Friday Evening Discourse delivered before the
Royal Institution, June 4, 1897.

BY

W. H. PREECE, C.B., F.R.S.

Reprinted from "The Electrician," June 11, 1897.

LONDON :
PRINTED BY GEORGE TUCKER, SALISBURY COURT, FLEET STREET, E.C.

SIGNALLING THROUGH SPACE WITHOUT WIRES*

Science has conferred one great benefit on mankind. It has supplied us with a new sense. We can now see the invisible, hear the inaudible, and feel the intangible. We know that the universe is filled with a homogeneous continuous elastic medium which transmits heat, light, electricity and other forms of energy from one point of space to another without loss. The discovery of the real existence of this 'ether' is one of the great scientific events of the Victorian era. Its character and mechanism are not yet known by us. All attempts to 'invent' a perfect ether have proved beyond the mental powers of the highest intellects. We can only say with Lord Salisbury that the ether is the nominative case to the verb 'to undulate.' We must be content with a knowledge of the fact that it was created in the beginning for the transmission of energy in all its forms, that it transmits these energies in definite waves and with a known velocity, that it is perfect of its kind, but that it still remains as inscrutable as gravity or life itself.

Any disturbance of the ether must originate with some disturbance of matter. One of the greatest scientific achievements of our generation is the magnificent generalization of Clerk-Maxwell that all these disturbances are of precisely the same kind, and that they differ only in degree. Light is an electromagnetic phenomenon, and electricity in its progress through space follows the laws of optics. Hertz proved this experimentally, and few of us who heard it will forget the admirable lecture on 'The Work on Hertz' given in this hall by Prof. Oliver Lodge three years ago.[†]

By the kindness of Prof. Silvanus Thompson I am able to illustrate wave transmission by a very beautiful apparatus devised by him. At one end we have the *transmitter* or oscillator, which is a heavy suspended mass to which a blow or impulse is given, and which, in consequence, vibrates a given number of times per minute. At the other end is the *receiver*, or resonator, timed to vibrate to the same period. Connecting the two together is a row of leaden balls suspended so that each ball gives a portion of its energy at each oscillation to the next in the series. Each ball vibrates at right angles to or athwart the line of propagation of the wave, and as they vibrate in different phases you will see that a wave is transmitted from the transmitter to the receiver. The receiver takes up these vibrations and responds in sympathy with the transmitter. Here we have a visible illustration of that which is absolutely invisible. The wave you see differs from a wave of light or of electricity only in its length or in its frequency. Electric waves vary from units per second in long submarine cables to millions per second when excited by Hertz's method. Light waves vary per second between 400 billions in

* Abstract of a Friday Evening Discourse delivered before the Royal Institution, 4 June 1897.
† This is published in an enlarged and useful form by the Electrician Printing and Publishing Company. – W.H.P.

the red to 800 billions in the violet, and electric waves differ from them in no other respect. They are reflected, refracted and polarized, they are subject to interference, and they move through the ether in straight lines with the same velocity, viz., 186,400 miles per second – a number easily recalled when we remember that is was in the year 1864 that Maxwell made his famous discovery of the identity of light and electric waves.

In 1884 messages sent through insulated wires buried in iron pipes in the streets of London were read upon telephone circuits erected on poles above the housetops, 80 ft away. Ordinary telegraph circuits were found in 1885 to produce disturbances 2,000 ft away. Distinct speech by telephone was carried on through one quarter of a mile, a distance that was increased to 1¼ mile at a later date. Careful experiments were made in 1886 and 1887 to prove that these effects were due to pure electromagnetic waves, and were entirely free from any earth-conduction. In 1892 distinct messages were sent across a portion of the British Channel between Penarth and Flat Holm, a distance of 3.3 miles.

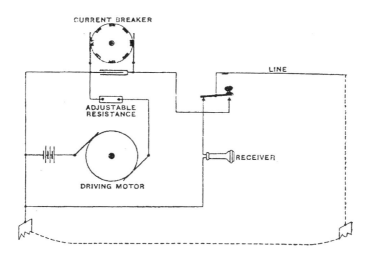

Fig. 1 Diagram of connections of Mr Preece's system

Early in 1885 the cable between Oban and the Isle of Mull broke down, and as no ship was available for repairing and restoring communication, communication was established by utilising parallel wires on each side of the Channel and transmitting signals across this space by these electromagnetic waves.

The apparatus (Fig. 1) connected to each wire consists of –

(a) A rheotome or make and break wheel, causing about 260 undulations per second in the primary wire.

(b) An ordinary battery of about 100 Leclanché cells, of the so-called dry and portable form.
(c) A Morse telegraph key.
(d) A telephone to act as receiver.
(e) A switch to start and stop the rheotome.

Good signals depend more on the rapid rise and fall of the primary current than on the amount of energy thrown into vibration. Leclanché cells give as good signals at 3.3 miles distant as 1½ H.P. transformed into alternating currents by an alternator, owing to the smooth sinusoidal curves of the latter. 260 vibrations per second give a pleasant note to the ear, easily read when broken up by the key into dots and dashes.

In my electromagnetic system two parallel circuits are established, one on each side of the channel or a bank of a river, each circuit becoming successively the primary and a secondary of an induction system, according to the direction in which these signals are being sent. Five miles of clear space have separated the two circuits.

Such effects have been known scientifically in the laboratory since the days of Faraday and of Henry, but it is only within the last few years that I have been able to utilise them practically through considerable distances. This has been rendered possible through the introduction of the telephone.

Last year (August, 1896) an effort was made to establish communication with the North Sandhead (Goodwin) lightship. The apparatus used was designed and manufactured by Messrs. Evershed and Vignoles, and a most ingenious relay to establish a call was invented by Mr Evershed. One extremity of the cable was coiled in a ring on the bottom of the sea, embracing the whole area over which the lightship swept while swinging to the tide, and the other end was connected with the shore. The ship was surrounded above the water line with another coil. The two coils were separated by a mean distance of about 200 fathoms, but communication was found to be impracticable. The screening effect of the sea water and the effect of the iron hull of the ship absorbed practically all the energy of the currents in the coiled cable, and the effects on board, though perceptible, were very trifling – too minute for signalling. Previous experiments had failed to show the extremely rapid rate at which energy is absorbed with the depth or thickness of sea water. The energy is absorbed in forming eddy currents. There is no difficulty whatever in signalling through 15 fathoms; speech by telephone has been maintained through 6 fathoms. Although this experiment has failed through water, it is thoroughly practical through air to considerable distances where it is possible to erect wires of similar length to the distance to be crossed on each side of the channel. It is not always possible, however, to do this, nor to get the requisite height to secure the best effect. It is impossible on a lightship

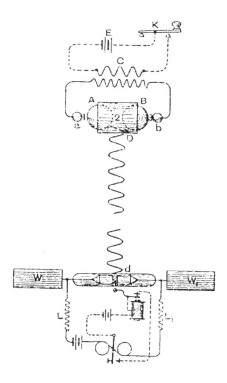

Fig. 2 Diagram of the Marconi apparatus

and on rock lighthouses. There are many small islands – Sark, for example – where it cannot be done.

In July last Mr Marconi brought to England a new plan. Mr Marconi utilises electric or Hertzian waves of very high frequency. He has invented a new relay which, for sensitiveness and delicacy, exceeds all known electrical apparatus.

The peculiarity of Mr Marconi's system is that, apart from the ordinary connecting wires of the apparatus, conductors of very moderate length only are needed, and even these can be dispensed with if reflectors are used.

The Transmitter – His transmitter is Prof. Righi's form of Hertz's radiator (Fig. 2).

Two spheres of *solid* brass, 4in in diameter (A and B), are fixed in an oil tight case D of insulating material, so that a hemisphere of each is exposed, the other hemisphere being immersed in a bath of vaseline oil. Mr Marconi uses generally waves of about 120 centimetres long. Two small spheres, *a* and *b*, are fixed close to the large spheres and connected each to one end of the secondary circuit of the 'induction coil' C, the primary circuit of which is excited by a battery E, thrown in and out of circuit by the Morse key K. Now, whenever the key K is depressed sparks pass between 1, 2 and 3, and since the system A B contains capacity and electric inertia, oscillations are set up in it of extreme rapidity. The

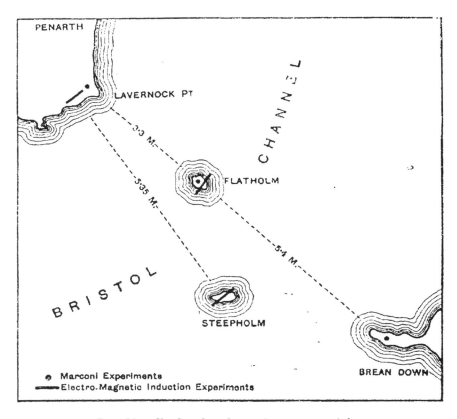

Fig. 3 Map of locality where the experiments were carried out

line of propagation is D*d*, and the frequency of oscillation is probably about 250 millions per second.

The distance at which effects are produced with such rapid oscillations depends chiefly on the energy in the discharge that passes. A 6in. spark coil has sufficed through 1, 2, 3, up to four miles, but for greater distances we have used a more powerful coil – one emitting sparks 20in long. It may also be pointed out that this distance increases with the diameter of the spheres A and B, and it is nearly doubled by making the spheres solid instead of hollow.

The Receiver – Marconi's relay (Fig. 2) consists of a small glass tube four centimetres long, into which two silver pole-pieces are tightly fitted, separated from each other by about half a millimeter – a thin space which is filled up by a mixture of fine nickel and silver filings, mixed with a trace of mercury. The tube is exhausted to a vacuum of 4mm, and sealed. It forms part of a circuit containing a local cell and a sensitive telegraph relay. In its normal condition the metallic powder is virtually an insulator. The particles lie higgledy-piggledy, anyhow in disorder. They lightly touch each other in an irregular method, but when electric waves fall upon them they are 'polarised,' order is installed. They are marshalled in serried ranks, they are subject to pressure – in fact, as Prof. Oliver Lodge expresses it, they 'cohere' – electrical contact ensues, and a current passes. The resistance of such a space falls from infinity to about five ohms. The electric resistance of Marconi's relay – that is, the resistance of the thin disc of loose powder – is practically infinite when it is in its normal or disordered condition. It is then, in fact, an insulator. This resistance drops sometimes to five ohms, when the absorption of the electric waves by it is intense. It therefore becomes a conductor. It may be, as suggested by Professor Lodge, that we have in the measurement of the variable resistance of this instrument a means of determining the intensity of the energy falling upon it. This variation is being investigated both as regards the magnitude of the energy and the frequency of the incident waves. Mons E. Branly (1890) showed this effect with copper, aluminium and iron filings. Prof. Oliver Lodge, who has done more than any one else in England to illustrate and popularise the work of Hertz and his followers, has given the name 'coherer' to this form of apparatus. Marconi 'decoheres' by making the local current very rapidly vibrate a small hammer head against the glass tube, which it does effectually, and in doing so makes such a sound that reading Morse characters is easy. The same current that decoheres can also record Morse signals on paper by ink. The exhausted tube has two wings which, by their size, tune the receiver to the transmitter by varying the capacity of the apparatus.* Choking coils prevent the energy The analogy to Prof. Silvanus Thompson's wave apparatus is evident. Oscillations set up in the transmitter fall upon the receiver tuned in sympathy with it, coherence follows, currents are excited, and signals made.

In open clear spaces within sight of each other nothing more is wanted, but when obstacles intervene and great distances are in question height is needed – tall masts, kites and balloons have been used. Excellent signals have been transmitted between Penarth and Brean Down, near Weston-super-Mare, across the Bristol Channel, a distance of nearly nine miles (Fig. 3). [The system was here shown in operation.]

Mirrors also assist and intensify the effects. They were used in the earlier experiments, but they have been laid aside for the present, for they are not only expensive to make, but they occupy much time in manufacture.

The wings shown in Fig. 2 may be removed. One pole can be connected with earth, and the other extended up to the top of the mast, or fastened to a balloon

---

* The period of vibration of a circuit is given by the equation $T = 2\pi \sqrt{KL}$, so that we have simply to vary either the capacity K or the so-called 'self-induction' L to tune the receiver to any frequency. It is simpler to vary K.

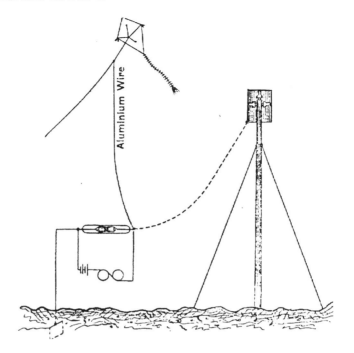

Aluminium Wire

Fig. 4 Diagram of Marconi connections when using pole or kite

by means of a wire. The wire and balloon or kite covered with tin foil becomes the wing. In this case one pole of the transmitter must also be connected with earth. This is shown by Fig. 4.

There are some apparent anomalies that have developed themselves during the experiments. Mr Marconi finds that his relay acts even when it is placed in a perfectly closed metallic box. This is the fact that has given rise to the rumour that he can blow up an ironclad ship. This might be true if he could plant his properly tuned receiver in the magazine of an enemy's ship.

The distance to which signals have been sent is remarkable. On Salisbury Plain Mr Marconi covered a distance of four miles. In the Bristol Channel this has been extended to over eight miles, and we have by no means reached the limit. It is interesting to read the surmises of others. Half a mile was the wildest dream.*

It is easy to transmit many messages in any direction at the same time. It is

---

* 'Unfortunately at present we cannot detect the electromagnetic waves more than 100 ft from their source.' – Trowbridge, 1897, 'What is Electricity,' page 256. 'If I mention 40 yards because that was one of the first out of the door experiments, but I should think that something more like half a mile was nearer the limit of sensibility. However, this is a rash statement not at present verified.' – Oliver Lodge, 1894, 'The Work of Hertz,' p. 18.

only necessary to tune the transmitters and receivers to the same frequency or 'note.' I could show this here, but we are bothered by reflection from the walls. This does not happen in open space. Tuning is very easy. It is simply necessary to vary the capacity of the receiver, and this is done by increasing the length of the wings W in Fig. 2. The proper length is found experimentally close to the transmitter. It is practically impossible to do so far away.

It has been said that Mr Marconi has done nothing new. He has not discovered any new rays; his transmitter is comparatively old; his receiver is based on Branly's coherer. Columbus did not invent the egg, but he showed how to make it stand on its end, and Marconi has produced from known means a new electric eye more delicate than any known electrical instrument, and a new system of telegraphy that will reach places hitherto inaccessible There are a great many practical points connected with this system that require to be threshed out in a practical manner before it can be placed on the market, but enough has been done to prove its value and to show that for shipping and lighthouse purposes it will be a great and valuable acquisition.

Marconi's review of his progress up to 1905

In 1899 Marconi read a paper, entitled 'Wireless Telegraphy', at the Institution of Electrical Engineers, London which outlined his original circuitry and summarised his activities up to that time both in Ireland and England (see Chapters 3 and 4). The paper itself was a sensation.[1]

By 1905 Marconi had made further considerable progress with transmitters/ receivers, especially receivers, together with comments on propagation etcetera. The paper entitled *Recent Advances in Wireless Telegraphy* was read at the Royal Institution, London and subsequently published in the proceedings.[2] It is reproduced in its entirety in this appendix.

It will be noted that the Marconi Station at Crookhaven (Chapter 6) is given significant prominence in the paper, in the context of the need for tuned circuit receivers to prevent interference on the 'omnibus' telegraph line between Cork and Crookhaven, originally constructed by Julius Reuter in 1863. It appears that there were a dozen or more telegraph offices, all with their instruments joined up to the same line, running from the terminal stations. It will be noted from the paper that Marconi put considerable effort into tuning receivers.

Perhaps one of the most important circuits that Marconi designed, patented and fabricated during 1902, was the Magnetic Detector. Based on an idea of Lord Rutherford, it acted as a receiver when a decrease in magnetic hysteresis takes place in magnetised iron exposed to high frequency or Hertzian waves. It was far more efficient, and accepted signals faster, than the coherer, and soon became a standard item in receivers for many years up to and including World War I. It is described in the 1905 paper and was commonly, if not affectionately, known as the 'Maggie'.

Marconi also discusses long distance propagation in the paper with its variations between day and night and carried out transmissions up to 2000 miles from Poldhu – the forerunner of his commercial venture between Clifden and Glace Bay. Work actually commenced on this undertaking in 1905.

---

1 G. Marconi, 'Wireless telegraphy', *Journal of the Institution of Electrical Engineers* 28/18, March 1899.
2 G. Marconi, 'Recent advances in wireless telegraphy', *Proceedings of the Royal Institution* 18/99, March 1905.

WEEKLY EVENING MEETING.

Friday, March 3, 1905.

His Grace the Duke of Northumberland, K.G. D.C.L. F.R.S.,
President, in the Chair.

Chevalier G. Marconi, LL.D. D.Sc. *M.R.I.*

Recent Advances in Wireless Telegraphy.

[ABSTRACT.]

THE phenomena of electro-magnetic induction, revealed chiefly by
the memorable researches and discoveries of Faraday carried out
in the Royal Institution, have long since shown how it is possible for
the transmission of electrical energy to take place across a small
air-space between a conductor traversed by a variable current and
another conductor placed near it ; and how such transmission may

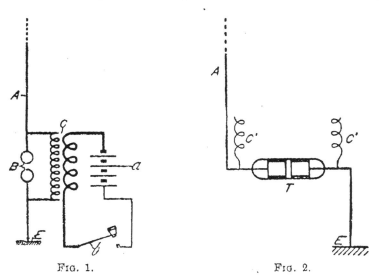

Fig. 1.   Fig. 2.

be detected and observed at distances greater or less, according to
the more or less rapid variation of the current in one of the wires,
and also according to the greater or less quantity of electricity brought
into play.

Maxwell, inspired by Faraday's work, gave to the world in 1873
his wonderful mathematical theory of electricity and magnetism,

demonstrating on theoretical grounds the existence of electro-magnetic waves, fundamentally similar to but enormously longer than waves of light. Following up Maxwell, Hertz in 1887 furnished his great practical proof of the existence of these true electro-magnetic waves.

Building on the foundations prepared by these great men, the author carried out in 1895 and 1896 his first tests, with apparatus

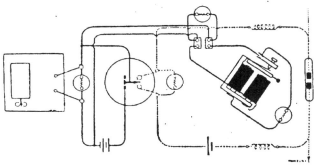

FIG. 3.

which embodied the principle on which long-distance wireless tele-graphy is successfully worked at the present day. This early arrange-ment is shown in Figs. 1, 2, and 3.

In Figs. 1 and 2 are shown diagrammatically the complete trans-mitting and receiving plants, and in Fig. 3 are shown the circuits of the receiving instruments.

The main feature of the system is the utilisation of the earth-effect by connecting both the transmitting and receiving instruments between earth and a raised capacity.

The later improvements introduced in the author's system of wireless telegraphy have been directed towards the following ends :—

1. To obtain independence of communication, or the prevention of interference between several neighbouring stations.

2. To increase the distance of communication.

3. To increase the efficiency of the apparatus, its accuracy and working speed.

One of the chief objections which is raised against wireless tele-graphy is that it is possible to work only two or a very limited number of stations in the immediate vicinity of each other without causing mutual interference, or producing a jumble by the confusion of the different messages. This objection appears to be much more serious to that section of the public which knows little or nothing of telegraphy in general than to telegraph engineers, who know that without organisation and discipline the same interference would occur in the great majority of ordinary land telegraphs. For example, there is an " omnibus " line between Cork and Crookhaven. On this

line there are a dozen or more telegraph offices, all with their instruments joined up to the same wire running from the terminal stations.
Now, if any of these offices should proceed to send a message, say, to
Cork, whilst this office is receiving another message from Crookhaven,
it would cause an interference which would result in the confusion of
the two messages, thus rendering them unintelligible.   Any message
sent on the line will affect all the instruments, and can be read by all
the other telegraph offices on the line ; but certain rules and regula-
tions are laid down, and adhered to by the operators in the employ
of the General Post Office, which make it impossible for one station
to interfere with the rest.   It is obvious that these same rules are
applicable to every case in which a group of equally tuned wireless
telegraph stations happen to be in proximity to each other.

Although in many instances untuned wireless telegraphy may
prove of great utility, it is, however, clear that, so long as some
method of rendering stations completely independent of one another
was not devised, a very important and effectual limit to the practical
utilisation of wireless telegraphy would be imposed.

The new method adopted by the author, in 1898, of connecting
a proper form of oscillation transformer in conjunction with a condenser (Fig. 4), so as to form a resonator tuned to respond best to

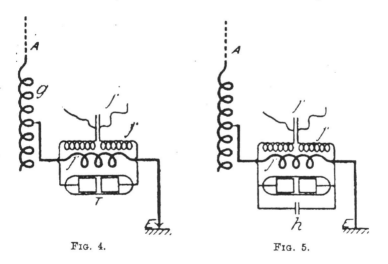

Fig. 4.   Fig. 5.

waves emitted by a given length of vertical wire, was a step in the
right direction.   This improvement was described by the author in a
discourse which he had the honour to deliver in the Royal Institution
in February 1900.

Apart, however, from these improvements introduced into the
receiving circuits, it had been for some time apparent that one

difficulty in the way of obtaining syntonic effects was caused by the
action of the transmitting wire. This straight rod or wire in which
electrical oscillations are set up, forms, as is well known, a very good
radiator or emitter of electric waves ; but, at the same time, in all
such good radiators, electrical oscillations set up by the ordinary
spark-discharge method cease, or are damped out very quickly by the
electrical radiation, which removes very rapidly the small amount of
their stored up energy.

It is well known that if two tuning forks are taken, having the
same periods of vibration or note, and one of them is set in motion
by striking it sharply, waves or sounds will form in the air ; and the
other tuning-fork, if in suitable proximity, will immediately com-
mence to vibrate, or sound in unison with the first.

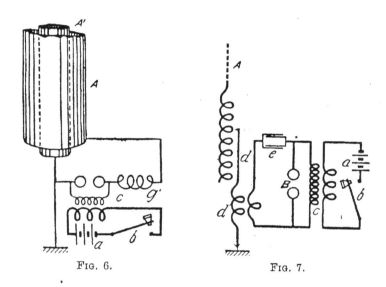

FIG. 6.   FIG. 7.

Of coarse, tuning-forks have to do with air waves, and wireless
telegraphy with ether waves, but the action in both cases is analogous.

There is one essential condition which must be fulfilled in order
that a well-marked tuning or electrical resonance may take place,
and it is based on the fact that what we call electrical resonance,
like mechanical resonance, depends essentially upon the accumulated
effect of a large number of feeble impulses properly timed. Tuning
can only be achieved if a sufficient number of these timed electrical
impulses reach the receiver.

Over four years ago, the author obtained satisfactory results by
increasing the electrical capacity of the radiating and resonating
conductors by arranging them at each station in the form of two

concentric cylinders, or in other forms of closely adjacent conductors. The electrical capacity of such conductors, as shown in Fig. 6, is very large compared with that of a single vertical wire, with the result that the amount of electrical energy stored up in the system referred to in the first case is much larger, and does not radiate or get away in one or two waves, but forms a train of timed impulses which subsist for a certain time, which is what is required.

An arrangement consisting of a circuit containing a condenser and a spark gap, Fig. 8, constitutes a very persistent oscillator.   Sir Oliver Lodge has shown that by placing it near to another similar circuit, it is possible to demonstrate effects of tuning.   The experiment is usually referred to as "Lodge's syntonic jars," and is extremely interesting, but as Lodge himself points out in his book, the "Work of Hertz," a closed circuit such as this is "a feeble radiator and a feeble absorber, so that it is not adapted for action at a distance."

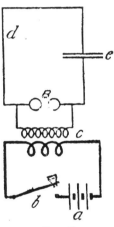

If, however, such an oscillating circuit is inductively associated with one of the author's elevated radiators, it is possible to cause the energy contained in the closed circuit to radiate to great distances, the essential condition being that the natural period of electrical oscillation of the radiator should be equal to that of the nearly closed circuit.

All the latest syntonic transmitting arrangements are based on modifications of this combination.

The general arrangement is indicated in Fig. 7.

The arrangements for syntonising or tuning the receiving stations are shown in Fig. 5.

FIG. 8.

Here is shown the usual vertical conductor connected to earth through the primary of a transformer, the secondary circuit of which contains a condenser, which is connected across the coherer or detector. In this case also it is necessary that the period of electrical oscillations of the vertical wire, which includes the primary of the transformer and earth connection, should be equal to that of, or in tune with, the secondary circuit of the said transformer, which circuit includes a condenser.   Therefore, in order that a transmitter (Fig. 7) should be in tune with the receiver (Fig. 5), it is necessary that the periods of oscillation of the several oscillating circuits at both stations should be equal, or very approximately so.

It is easy to understand that if we have several stations, each tuned to a different period of electrical oscillation, the periods of resonance of which are known, it will not be difficult to transmit

messages to any one of them without the signals being picked up by
the other stations for which they are not intended. It is obvious
that the greater the difference in periods of the oscillation or tune
between two stations, the smaller will be the possibility of tapping
and mutual interference.

It is also possible to connect to one sending wire, through the

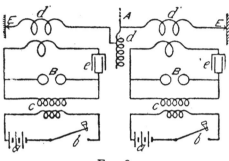

FIG. 9.

connections of different inductances, several differently tuned transmitters, and to a receiving wire a number of corresponding receivers,
as is shown in Figs. 9 and 10.

It was possible, nearly five years ago, to send different messages
simultaneously without interference, the messages being received on
differently tuned receivers connected to the same vertical conductor.

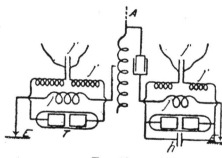

FIG. 10.

This result was described in the *Times* of October 4, 1900, by
Professor Fleming, who, in company with others, witnessed the test.

A recent improvement introduced in the method of tuning the
receiver is that shown in Fig. 11.

There exists at present among a large section of the public considerable misconception as to the feasibility of tuning or syntonising

wireless telegraphic installations, and also as to what is generally termed "the interception of messages." According to the accepted understanding, "intercepting" a message means or implies securing by force, or by other means, a communication which is intended for somebody else, thereby preventing the intended recipient from receiving it. Now this is just what has never happened in the case of wireless telegraphy. It is quite true that messages are, and have been, tapped or overheard at stations for which they are not intended, but this does not by any means prevent the messages from reaching their proper destination. Of course, if a powerful transmitter giving off strong waves of different frequencies is actuated near one of the receiving stations, it may prevent the reception of messages, but the party working the so-called interfering station is at the same time unable to read the message he is trying to destroy, and therefore,

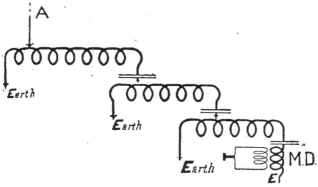

Fig. 11.

the message is not, in the popular sense of the word, "intercepted." It should be remembered that any telegraph or telephone wire can be tapped, or the conversation going on through it overheard, or its operation interfered with. Sir William Preece has published results which go to show that it is possible to pick up at a distance on another circuit, the conversation which may be passing through a telephone or telegraph wire.

Up to the commencement of 1902, the only receivers that could be practically employed for the purposes of wireless telegraphy were based on what may be called the coherer principle—that is, the detector, the principle of which is based on the discoveries and observations made by S. A. Varley, Professor Hughes, Calsecchi Onesti, and Professor Branly.

Early in that year the author was fortunate enough to succeed in constructing a practical receiver of electric waves, based on a principle different from that of the coherer. Speaking from the experience of its application for over two years to commercial purposes, the author is able to say that, in so far as concerns speed of working, facility of adjustment, reliability and efficiency when used on tuned circuits, this receiver has left all coherers or anti-coherers far behind.

The action of this receiver is in the author's opinion based upon the decrease of magnetic hysteresis which takes place in iron, when under certain conditions this metal is exposed to high frequency oscillations or Hertzian waves.

It is constructed in the following manner and is shown in Fig. 12.

On an insulating sleeve surrounding a portion of a core, consisting of an endless rope of thin iron wires, are wound one or two layers of thin insulated copper wires. Over this winding insulating material is placed, and over this again another longer winding of thin copper wire contained in a narrow bobbin. The ends of the windings nearer the iron core are connected one to earth and the other to the elevated

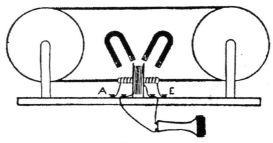

FIG. 12.

conductor, or they may be joined to any suitable syntonising circuit, such as is now employed for syntonic wireless telegraphy. The ends of the longer winding are connected to the terminals of a suitable telephone. A pair of horse-shoe magnets are conveniently disposed for magnetising the portion of the core surrounded by the windings, and the endless iron core is caused to move continuously through the windings and the field of the horse-shoe magnets.

This detector is and has been successfully employed for both long and short distance work. It is used on the ships of the Royal Navy and on all transatlantic liners which are carrying on a long-distance news service. It has also been used to a large extent in the tests across the Atlantic Ocean.

As already stated, the adoption of this magnetic receiver was the means of bringing about a great improvement in the practical working conditions of wireless telegraphy, by making it possible to do away with the troublesome adjustments necessary when using coherers, and also by considerably increasing the speed at which it is possible to receive, the speed depending solely on the ability of the individual operators. Thus a speed of over thirty words a minute has been easily attained with the apparatus as shown in Fig. 12.

This form of magnetic receiver, however, presented a disadvantage which some people considered very important—of being able to bring about only an audible reproduction of the signals in a telephone, and consequently ineffective for actuating a recording instrument, such as would leave a documentary proof in the form of Morse signals received and inscribed on tape.

When the author had the honour to deliver his last lecture at the Royal Institution, he expressed a hope that by means of this magnetic receiver it might be possible to work a recording instrument, and he is glad to be able to announce that he has recently been able to construct a magnetic receiver that will work a relay and a recorder.

The causes which prevented the author's earlier type of magnetic receiver from working a relay were the rapidity and alternating character of the current induced by the effect of the oscillations on the iron. This current or impulse is so sudden that, although it proves to be suitable in producing a sound or click in a telephone diaphragm, it is far too quick to impart any appreciable movement to the comparatively heavy tongue of a relay, and in that way to allow a current to work a recording or other instrument. By modifying the circuits, especially by increasing their length and by the use of a particular quality of iron, the author has been able to obtain an impulse from the magnetic receiver, which is capable of working a recording instrument.

The instrument is eminently adapted for receiving messages from stations such as Poldhu, where the length of wave radiated is considerable.

The advantages of this receiver over the coherer system of receiver are very great.

In the first place, it is far more simple, requires far less attention, is absolutely reliable and constant in its action, and possesses a low and unvarying resistance. But the chief advantage lies in the fact that with this receiver it is possible to attain a very high speed of working.

The speed of the author's earlier form of magnetic receivers was limited to the rate at which the operator could read by sound. So far as speed is concerned, however, this new detector is not dependent upon the ability of the operator. It is possible to use an automatic transmitter to send messages at the rate of 100 words a minute, and the messages will be picked up and recorded quite clearly and distinctly by means of this new form of receiver.

The author here gave a demonstration of wireless transmission and reception by means of high speed "Wheatstone" instruments lent by the G.P.O., used in conjunction with his magnetic receiver.

This form of recording receiver has been satisfactorily worked over a distance of 152 miles over land, and will shortly be employed in connection with the new transatlantic stations.

In conjunction with Professor Fleming, the author has recently introduced further improvements which greatly increase the efficiency of the apparatus, but which he is not at present free to describe. The author here demonstrated the effect of the improvement by means of a galvanometer, showing the deflection without and with the new device. The author also exhibited and explained Dr. Fleming's cymometer for measuring the length of waves used in wireless telegraphy.*

A very considerable amount of public interest has been centred during the last few years on the tests and experiments in which the author has been engaged in investigating the possibilities of wireless telegraphy over very great distances, and especially on the tests which are being carried out across the Atlantic Ocean.

The facility with which distances of over 200 miles could be covered with the author's apparatus as long ago as 1900, and the knowledge that by means of syntonic devices mutual interferences could be prevented, led the author to advise the construction of two large power stations, one in Cornwall and the other in North America, in order to test whether, by the employment of much greater power, it might not be possible to transmit messages across the Atlantic Ocean.

On the erection of these stations very extensive tests and experiments were carried out during the latter part of 1902. These tests were greatly facilitated by the courtesy of the Italian Government, which placed a 7000-ton cruiser, the *Carlo Alberto*, at the author's disposal. During these trials the interesting fact was observed that, unlike what occurs with moderate power-transmitting stations, the effect of intervening land or mountains between the sending and receiving apparatus does not bring about any considerable reduction in the distances over which it is possible to communicate; this result being due, no doubt, to the much greater length of wave radiated by the big elevated conductor of the long-distance stations, compared with the shorter wave-length radiated by the smaller and less powerful installations. Thus messages were received from Poldhu at the positions marked on the map (Fig. 13), which is a copy of the map accompanying the official report of the experiments. These positions, at which signals were received direct from Poldhu, are in the Baltic near Sweden, at Kiel, the North Sea, the Bay of Biscay, also Ferrol, Cadiz, Gibraltar, Sardinia, and Spezia. Messages were received distinctly in these places from Cornwall, although, in the Baltic, the whole of England, the Netherlands, and part of Germany and Scandinavia lay between Poldhu and the *Carlo Alberto*. Also, at Cadiz and Gibraltar, the whole of Spain

* Dr. J. A. Fleming, "On an Instrument for the Measurement of the Length of Long Electric Waves and also Small Inductances and Capacities." *Proc. Roy. Soc. Lond.*, vol. lxxiv.

intervened ; and at Spezia and Cagliari, in the Mediterranean, the whole of France, including the Alps, lay in a direct line between the two stations.

After these experiments the *Carlo Alberto* was sent back from the Mediterranean to Plymouth, and thence conveyed the author to Canada ; and in October 1902 signals from Poldhu were received on board ship throughout the voyage up to a distance of 2300 miles.

In December 1902 messages were exchanged between the stations at Poldhu and Cape Breton, but it was found that communication was better from Canada to England than in the opposite direction.

The reason for this is to be attributed to the fact that, owing to the support and encouragement of the Canadian Government, the station at Cape Breton had been more efficiently and more expensively equipped ; whilst as regards Poldhu, owing to the uncertainty as to what would be the attitude of the British Government at that

FIG. 13.

time towards the working of the station, the author's company was unwilling to expend large sums of money for the purpose of increasing its range of transmission.

As, however, messages were sent with ease and accuracy from Canada to England, the author considered it his duty to send the first messages to their Majesties the Kings of England and Italy, both of whom had previously given him much encouragement and assistance in his work. The author was thus enabled to announce that the transmission of telegraphic messages across the Atlantic Ocean without the use of cable or wire was an accomplished fact. Messages were also sent to His Majesty from Lord Minto, the Governor-General of Canada, who had taken a considerable interest in the author's early experiments in Canada. Officers delegated by the Italian Government, and a representative of the London *Times*, were present at the transmission of the messages, and over

2000 words were sent and correctly received in the presence of these Government delegates.

Further tests were then carried out at the long-distance station erected at Cape Cod, in the United States of America, and a message from President Roosevelt was successfully transmitted from this station to His Majesty the King.

In the spring of 1903 the transmission of news messages from America to the London *Times* was attempted, and the first messages were correctly received and published in that newspaper. A breakdown in the insulation of the apparatus at Cape Breton made it necessary, however, to suspend the service, and, unfortunately, further accidents made the transmission of messages unreliable, especially during the spring and summer. In consequence of this, the author's company decided not to attempt the transmission of any more public messages until such time as a reliable and continuous service could be maintained and guaranteed under all ordinary conditions.

It is curious to note that the transmission of messages across the Atlantic appeared to be much easier during the winter months of December, January and February, than during the spring and summer, but no serious difficulties were encountered before April. These were partly caused by the insulation of the aerial not being so good during the damp spring weather, when the snow and ice are melting and thawing, as at this period the insulation is much more difficult to maintain in an efficient condition than during the dry and crisp Canadian winter.

A new station, supplied with more powerful and more perfect apparatus, is in course of erection, and the author has not the slightest doubt but that in a very short time the practicability and reliability of transatlantic wireless telegraphy will be fully demonstrated.

In connection with these very powerful stations, it is interesting to observe that the fact which the author had noticed in 1895, and which he expressed in his patent of June 2, 1896, that "the larger the plates (or capacities) of the receiver and transmitter, and the higher from the earth the plates are suspended, the greater the distance that it is possible to communicate at parity of other conditions," still holds good, and therefore, the elevated conductors at these stations are much larger and higher than those used at the smaller power stations. The potential to which they are charged is also very much in excess of that used at the short-distance stations.

Pending the reconstruction of these long-distance stations, valuable tests have been carried out, and daily commercial work is carried on over distances of about 2000 miles. In October 1903, it was found possible to supply the Cunard ss. *Lucania* during her entire crossing from New York to Liverpool with news transmitted direct to that ship from Poldhu and Cape Breton.

Since June a regular long-distance commercial service has been in operation on certain ships of the Cunard Steamship Company, which ships, throughout their voyage across the Atlantic, receive daily news messages collected for transmission by Messrs. Reuter in England, and by the Associated Press in America. At present five transatlantic steamships are thus publishing a daily newspaper containing telegraphic messages of the latest news.

The practical and experimental work carried out in connection with the long- and short-distance stations has afforded valuable opportunities for noting and studying various unknown and unexpected effects of the condition of space on the propagation of electro-magnetic waves.

The author being able to avail himself of the daily reports of over 70 ships and 50 land stations, the chances of error from what might be termed accidental results are reduced to a minimum. Thus it is interesting to observe that the difference between the propagation of the wave by day and by night is only noticeable in the case of long-distance stations ; or, in other words, where a considerable amount of energy is forced into the transmitting aerial wires. For instance, all the short-distance ship-to-shore stations having a range of about 150 miles, averaged the same distance of communication by day as by night ; but the long-distance stations, such as Poldhu, Cape Breton and Cape Cod, as originally constructed, averaged by day two-fifths of the distance covered by night.

The opinion has been expressed that the reason for shorter distances being covered by day is due to the electrons propagated into space by the sun, and that if these are continually falling like a shower upon the earth, in accordance with the hypothesis of Professor Arrhenius, then that portion of the earth's atmosphere which is facing the sun will have in it more electrons than the part which is not facing the sun, and therefore it may be less transparent to long Hertzian waves.

The full scientific explanation of this fact has not yet been given, but Professor J. J. Thomson has shown in an interesting paper in the *Philosophical Magazine** that if electrons are distributed in a space traversed by long electric waves, these will tend to move the electrons in the direction of the wave, and will therefore absorb some of the energy of the wave. Hence, as Professor Fleming has pointed out in his Cantor Lectures delivered at the Society of Arts, a medium through which electrons or ions are distributed acts as a slightly turbid medium to long electric waves.

In fact, clear sunlight or blue skies, though very transparent to light-waves, may act as a fog to Hertzian waves. Apparently the amplitude of the electrical oscillations radiated has much to do with the interesting phenomenon, for the author has found that if a considerable amount of power is applied to the radiating apparatus of the so-called short distance stations, the difference between the range

---

* Vol. iv. Series 6, August 1902.

of transmission by night and by day becomes at once apparent, although no difference is made in the wave length radiated.

A curious feature of what may be called the daylight effect is the suddenness with which it may cut off the signals at great distances. These do not, as might be supposed, die off gradually as daylight increases, but seem to fade away rapidly, and disappear entirely within the space of about two minutes.

The author does not for a moment think that this daylight effect will prove to be a serious drawback to the practical application of long-distance wireless telegraphy, as its result amounts to this, that rather more power is required by day than by night to send signals by means of electric waves over long distances.

It has been stated that one of the serious objections to wireless telegraphy lay in the fact that no means existed for directing the energy emitted by the stations. If we assume this fact to be correct, we certainly find that, if it presents certain disadvantages, it also presents many perhaps counterbalancing advantages. For example, if a cable is laid between England and Canada it can only serve for communication between these two countries; but if a wireless connection is established between two such countries the stations may be instantly used in time of war, or in any other emergency, to communicate with other stations, situated say, at Gibraltar, the West Indies, or some inland point in North America, and also, if necessary, with warships carrying apparatus tuned to the waves such stations radiate. By means of syntony, although the energy cannot be directed in one direction, it can however be picked up at certain distances only by certain tuned receivers, as occurs now with the ships crossing the ocean. Fifty of these ships carry wireless apparatus, but only five of them have the instrument tuned to receive the long-distance news messages sent from Poldhu; and, as a matter of fact, these messages are received only by those five specially tuned ships.

Before concluding, it may not be out of place to give a few details as to the practical uses to which the author's system of wireless telegraphy has already been put.

There are now over 80 British and 30 Italian warships equipped. A number of these warships are fitted with long-distance apparatus, and are therefore able to keep in touch with England when far out on the Atlantic, at Gibraltar, and in the Mediterranean. Admiral Lord Charles Beresford has authorised the author to say that during the last cruise of the Channel Fleet from Gibraltar to England they had no difficulty whatever in receiving messages from Cornwall during the entire voyage by means of special long-distance receivers.

Seventy liners, belonging respectively to England, Italy, France, Germany, Holland, Belgium, and the United States, are fitted with the author's apparatus, and are engaged in carrying on commercial work for the benefit of passengers between ship and ship and between ship and shore; and for this latter purpose there are over 50 land stations with which to communicate.   During 1904, 67,625 commercial messages were sent and received at the ship and shore stations controlled by the author's company.

It is also used as a branch of the Italian telegraphic system for ordinary commercial purposes across the Adriatic Sea, namely, between Bari (in Italy) and Antivari (in Montenegro), and in the Straits of Messina at Messina, Reggio and Giovanni.   Also, in connection with the British Post Office, from Cornwall to the Scilly Islands, on the not infrequent occasions of the breaking down of the cables.

As to the future of wireless telegraphy, the author expresses his confidence in its ability to furnish a more economical means for the transmission of telegrams from England to America, and from England to the Colonies, than the present service carried on by the cables.

It is true that many scientific men are dubious of the practicability of sending electric waves to great distances.   Others are not. On a recent memorable occasion at Glasgow University, Lord Kelvin publicly stated that he not merely believed that messages could be transmitted across the Atlantic, but that some day it would be possible to send messages to the other side of the globe.   Apart from the practical and economical possibilities of this step, when realised, the transmission of messages to the Antipodes would open up the possibility of carrying out tests of very great scientific interest.   For example, if transmission to the Antipodes were possible, the energy ought to go over or travel round all parts of the globe from one station to the other, and perhaps concentrate at the Antipodes, and in this way it might perhaps be possible for messages to be sent to such distant lands by means of a very small amount of electrical energy, and, therefore, at a correspondingly small expense.

[G. M.]

Marconi's Nobel lecture, December 1909

This lecture, presented before a distinguished general audience, including the King of Sweden, shows the progressive sophistication of Marconi's development of wireless systems up to 1909.

A strange feature is that numerous textual alterations in Marconi's own handwriting are present throughout the entire text and the first page is actually signed by Marconi on 10 December 1909, i.e. just one day before the presentation itself.

Although some knowledge of electrical theory may be desirable for adequate understanding, there is no mistaking Marconi's mastering of his subject and what he had produced in twelve years beginning at the Villa Griffone in 1895 and culminating in the 'great commercial leap' over the Atlantic Ocean in 1907 with the powerful station at Clifden, Co. Galway.

In the concluding remarks, Marconi emphasises the safety factor associated with ships (the *Titanic* disaster was still to come) and 'foresaw the importance in furnishing efficient and economical communication between distant parts of the world'. This did not really occur on a large scale until the 1920s with short radio waves, but Marconi was discussing it approximately fifteen years before it was commercialised. Indeed at that stage Marconi was confidently predicting television and be became a leading world figure in this area in the 1930s along with precision navigational aids which could fairly be described as the origins of radar.

The initial pages are reproduced here. A facsimile of the typescript of the complete lecture with annotations by the author has been published by the Fondazione Guglielmo Marconi, Villa Griffone, Via Celestini, 1-40044, Pontecchio (BO), Italy.

*Lecture delivered at the Royal Academy of Science,
Stockholm, on 11th December, 1909.*

BY

COMMENDATORE G. MARCONI, LL.D., D.Sc.,

*On the occasion of the award to him of a Nobel Prize
for Physics.*

The discoveries connected with the
propagation of electric waves over long distances, and
the practical applications of telegraphy through space,
which have gained for me the high honour of sharing
the Nobel prize for Physics, have been made to a great extent
the result of one another.

The application of electric waves
to the purposes of wireless telegraphic communication
between distant parts of the earth, and the experiments
which I have been fortunate enough to carry out on a
larger scale than is attainable in ordinary laboratories,
have made it possible to investigate phenomena and note
results often novel and unexpected.

In my opinion many facts connected with the

~~propagation~~ *Transmission* of electric waves over great distances still

await a satisfactory explanation, and I hope to be able in

this Lecture to refer to some observations which appear to

require the attention of physicists.

In sketching the history of my association with

Radio Telegraphy, I might mention that I never studied

Physics or electrotechnics in the regular manner, although

as a boy I was deeply interested in those subjects.

I did however attend one course of lectures on

Physics under the late Professor Rosa at Livorno, and i was

the publications of that time dealing with

what I might say fairly well acquainted with scientific subject

including the works of Herts, Branly and Righi.|...|

Bibliography

For the reader interested in further pursuing the career of Marconi, a vast corpus of writings exists both in Italian and in English. The following list of publications, whilst not fully comprehensive, is, however, indicative of Marconi's achievements (publications referred to in the main text are not included).

There are several centres where Marconi archives are located. The Centro Internazionale per la Storia delle Università e delle Scienza (CIS) at Bologna (Professors Pancaldi and Guagini) together with the Fondazione Guglielmo Marconi at the Villa Griffone (Dr B. Valotti) and the Marconi Archives at GEC-Marconi, Chelmsford, UK are noteworthy sources.

Aiken, Hugh G.J., *Syntony and spark: the origins of radio* (New York: John Wiley and Sons, 1976).

Baker, W.J., *A history of the Marconi Company* (London: Methuen, 1970).

De Sousa, L., *Wireless telegraphy, 1895–1919: some personal experiences of its inception, development and achievements* (GEC-Marconi Archives). (Sig. De Sousa was Marconi's private secretary, 1915–22.)

Di Benedetto, G. and M. Bresadola, *Bibliografia Marconiana* (Firenze: Giunti Barbera, 1974).

Dunlap, Orrin E. Jr., *Marconi the man and his wireless* (New York: Macmillan, 1937).

Fahie, J.J., *A history of wireless telegraphy* (New York: Arno Press, 1901–71).

Falciasecca, G. and B. Valotti (eds), *Guglielmo Marconi, genio, storia & modernità* (Mondadori, Milano, 2003).

Fleming, J.A., *Memories of a scientific life* (London: Marshall, Morgan and Scott, 1934).

—— *Sui metodi con i quail l'irradiazione di onhe electriche puó essere limitata a particulari direzione* in *Scritti di Guglielmo Marconi* (Roma: Reale Accademia d'Italia, 1906), pp 153–6. (Fleming's development of the directional antenna was absolutely essential for the Clifden station to ensure that sufficient radio power reached Newfoundland.)

Garratt, G.R., *The early history of radio from Faraday to Marconi* (London: IEE/Science Museum, 1994).

Headrick, Daniel, *The invisible weapon: telecommunications and international politics, 1951–45* (Oxford: Oxford University Press, 1991).

Jacob, B.L., and D.M.B. Collier, *Marconi, master of space: an authorized biography of the Marchese Marconi* (London: Hutchinson, 1935).

Jolly, W.P., *Marconi* (London: Constable, 1972).

MacLaurin, W.R., *Invention and innovation in the radio industry* (New York: Macmillan, 1949).

O'Hara, J.G. and – Pricha, *Hertz and the Maxwilliams* (London: Peter Peregrinus/IEE, 1987).

Reade, L., *Marconi and the discovery of wireless* (London: Faber and Faber, 1963).

Ridella, F., *Guglielmo Marconi e il suo maestro di elettrotecnica Vincenzo Rosa* (Torino: SEI, 1941).

Rowlands, P. and J. Wilson (eds), *Oliver Lodge and the invention of radio* (Liverpool: PD Publications, 1994).

Solari, L., *Storia della radio* (Milano: Fratelli Treves, 1939). (Solari's detactor was used at Signal Hill for the transmission in December 1921.)

Valotti, B., and M. Bigazzi, *The roots of invention: new sources on young Marconi* (Bologna: *Universitas* no. 7, pp. 1–5, 1995).

Vyvyan, Richard N., *Wireless over thirty years* (London: Routledge, 1933). (Vyvyan was a senior technician with Marconi.)

Weightman, Gavin, *Signor Marconi's Magic Box: how an amateur inventor defied scientists and began the radio revolution* (London: HarperCollins, 2004).

Index